D1527601

MT
35
.M56
1991

MUSIC
MANUSCRIPT
PREPARATION:
a concise guide

by
Mona Mender

12 - 91

The Scarecrow Press, Inc.
Metuchen, N.J., & London
1991

035610

CONCORDIA COLLEGE LIBRARY
BRONXVILLE, N. Y. 10708

British Library Cataloguing-in-Publication data available

Library of Congress Cataloging-in-Publication Data

Mender, Mona, 1926-
    Music manuscript preparation : a concise guide / by   Mona Mender.
       p.   cm.
    Includes bibliographical references (p.
    ISBN 0-8108-2294-6 (alk. paper)
    1. Musical notation.   I. Title.
    MT35.M56   1991
    780.26'2—dc20   90-8373

Copyright © 1991 by Mona Mender
Manufactured in the United States of America

Printed on acid-free paper

ACKNOWLEDGMENTS

To Judy, Lynn, Don, and Irv for their faith in this project;

A special thanks to my husband for his patience, understanding, and support;

To Allen Bonde for the contribution of his expertise, encouragement, and enthusiastic cooperation;

To Alexander Caemmerer for strengthening my resolve;

To June Roth for guiding me through the whole process.

CONTENTS

Contents

FOREWORD

Every composer hopes to be able to write music anywhere, anytime—without needing a music library nearby for guidance in preparing a music manuscript. This is particularly true when composing contemporary music with unfamiliar formats and symbols. It is possible to create a legible, correct, and inviting manuscript for any composition by using this guide.

This book contains instructions and examples for proper preparation of manuscripts without the large expense of hiring a copyist. Any musician or group of musicians should then be able to perform compositions without explanation by the composer. This will save much time and energy for everyone and spare the composer rejection by the performers, critics, and teachers because of illegibility.

Mona Mender
Basking Ridge, N.J.

PART I: MATERIALS AND EQUIPMENT

A. PEN AND PENCIL

1. A pencil (#2) may be used for the initial drawing of the notation, bar lines, etc.

2. It is desirable to use a pliable pen with a fine point which will broaden when pressed and become fine again when the pressure is lessened and the angle at which it is held is changed. However, for the copyist not skilled in the use of this, a Probate stub pen point #313 (Esterbrook) and an oval pen point #788 (Esterbrook) used with a pen holder might be better. These points are not as flexible, therefore, not as sensitive to wrong pressures. They are easily available in stationery stores and other supply stores.

3. Medium points are preferred when the lines of the staff are widely spaced. Fine points are used for smaller spacing of lines such as those found in scores. "Speedball" pen point #5 and holder produces good results for bold lettering.

4. The **Osmiroid** "Music Writing Point" is flexible, but perhaps a bit too much so for the inexperienced.

5. The **Osmiroid** "Italic Medium" is good.

6. The **Platignum** pen (fountain type) is very good. Waterproof and Indian ink are *not* to be used with this pen or with any type of fountain pen.

7. A draftsman's ruling pen may be used for drawing straight lines. The width of the line is controlled and may be changed.

B. INK

1. The ink must be intensely black, free-flowing, heavy and opaque. Waterproof ink and India ink should be used with dip pens, never with the fountain type, since they are likely to clog the pen.

2. Brands

   a. **Monarch** Music Writing Ink (Carl Fischer Co., New York City) is good. When used with a fountain pen, it must be washed out very often to prevent clogging.

   b. **Higgins** Engrossing Ink is very black and flows nicely. This too may be used with a fountain pen but must be washed out very often.

   c. **Pelikan** is good. This may be used with a fountain pen but must be washed out often.

   d. **Higgins "Eternal"** (Carbon) #812 may leave a powder which may smudge.

   e. **FW Non-clogging Waterproof** Drawing Ink (black) is very good, but it can be used only with dip pens.

3. Cleaning materials

   a. Warm water

   b. **Higgins** Pen Cleaner is good for extra cleaning periodically.

   c. Fine emery board or sand paper for smoothing pen points.

   d. A small brush.

C. PAPER

1. Opaque manuscript paper is suitable for a working copy. A firm paper is desirable for a clear result.

2. Transparencies (translucent manuscript paper) are used for the final preparation before having it reproduced professionally. (The notation is placed on the blank side so that erasures do not include staff lines.)

3. The paper most used has twelve staves, since groups of two, three, four, or six staves can be accommodated. Double sheets are sold in many combinations: 8/10 (8 staves on one sheet, 10 on the other), 10/10, 10/12, 12/12, 9/12 and 12/12 (for 3 stave groupings), etc.

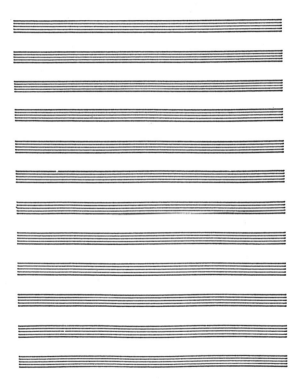

4. Song paper usually has groups of three staves. Two are connected by a brace for the piano part. It is desirable to have the vocal part far enough above the piano part to allow for the words which appear under the vocal line.

There is special paper with extra space between the vocal
and piano part. The paper should be of medium size so that
singers can handle it easily.

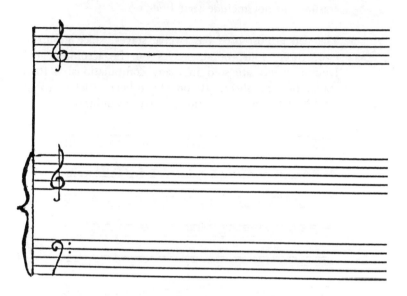

5. Organ music requires groups of three staves. Two staves
for the manuals are connected by a brace. Below these is
the third staff for the pedal part.

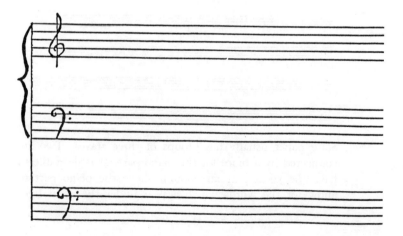

6. Quartet music naturally requires groups of four staves (unless one instrument uses double or triple staves). There are no brackets to join the staves, generally.

7. Piano music and other music which utilizes ledger lines require paper which has staves far enough apart from each other to allow for this.

8. Paper for full score usually has twenty-four staves, although larger sizes may be obtained.

9. Paper with different groupings of staves is available, but there is more freedom in doing one's own barring, bracing, bracketing, and listing of instruments before each staff.

10. Sizes of paper

    a. 9½″ × 12½″ or 11″ × 13½″ for solos and parts for concert band music, chamber music, and orchestral music. This paper usually has twelve staves.

    b. 5½″ × 6″ for parts in music for marching bands. These parts are smaller since they are usually clipped onto the instruments while marching.

11. *See* page 51 for information on layouts.

D. RULER

Cork-lined rulers, one measuring twelve inches and one shorter, are desirable because the cork raises the ruler away from the page, thus avoiding the wet ink. Metal rulers keep smoother edges than do plastic rulers, but the clear plastic ones have the advantage of being transparent.

E. BLOTTER

The blotter is not used to blot the transparency that is used for duplication. The printing will be pale from the blotting. It is used to lighten a mistake immediately so that it will be easier to erase.

F. ERASER

  1. A soft pencil eraser.

  2. An electric eraser. (Dietzgen Corp. makes a very good one. Many professionals use Brunning Electric Eraser.) This is a worthwhile investment. The soft white eraser should be chosen.

  3. A cement eraser is used for the residue of liquid rubber cement.

  4. Correction tape is available which has single staves with gum on the back. It is called "goof strips" or "patching tape."

G. SCOTCH TAPE AND CEMENT

  1. **Magic Transparent Tape #810** or **#8** may be used when cutting out a piece of paper and inserting another. This may be done with a razor against a ruler. (*See* page 63.)

  2. Liquid rubber cement is used to paste corrected bits of music on to opaque paper directly over mistakes. **Elmer's Glue-All** is satisfactory as well.

H. RAZOR BLADE (single-edged)

This blade can be used with a ruler for cutting translucent paper. It is also used to scratch out mistakes when the ink is dry. This is not always satisfactory, but worth a try on small mistakes.

I. OPTIONAL MATERIALS

    1. Lettering aids.

    2. Music typewriters and standard typewriters.

    3. A lettering triangle.

    4. Decals. These may be purchased in a shop having drafts-man's supplies. However, these are expensive.

    5. Flexible curves for drawing phrase marks, etc. are helpful. To help avoid smearing, a ruling pen is suggested.

    6. A compass for curves.

    7. A protractor for curves, straight lines, and exact measurements.

    8. A triangle with a bevelled edge.

    9. A cardboard folder.

   10. Masking tape for binding scores.

   11. Rubber stamp sets with the names of instruments, as well as rubber stamp kits for letters in titles, authors, etc.

   12. Scissors.

   13. A dictionary for proper hyphenation of words in the lyrics.

PART II: NOTATION

A. IMPORTANT RULES FOR NOTATION

1. A bar at the end of a line must not be broken.

2. A line must not start with a repeat sign.

3. Room must be left at the end of a page for a page turn.

4. A measure count must be taken. (*See* Proofreading, page 118.)

5. The pen should be held with a relaxed hand.

6. Clarity is the most important ingredient.

B. NOTE-HEADS

1. The note-head is an ellipse, pointing upward to the right: ○

2. The size of the note-head is determined by the space between the lines of the staff. If the staff lines are turned so that they are vertical and on top of the horizontal lines of the staff, one can visualize the ellipse of the note-head filling the square.

3. Grace and cue note-heads are much smaller. They are the same shape as normal-sized note-heads. (Small size notes or reversed notes may be used to clarify the strands of an intricate texture.)

4. A half-note is shaded differently from a whole-note:

half-note  whole-note

5. Spacing of notes and rests must coincide with that of accompanying parts. However, in a single line, the amount of space after a note usually reflects the length of time the note represents.

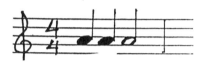

6. A whole-note may not be used to indicate a whole measure if there are more than four quarters. The whole-note is placed at the beginning of the measure. (A whole-rest may be used for the measure regardless of the meter signature and is placed in the middle of the bar.)

7. Spoken notes are indicated by marking a cross on the stem of a note (*see* VOCAL MUSIC, page 76). One method of notating the spoken notes is to use a single line and approximate the pitch of the spoken word; another method is to use one space on a staff, or approximate pitches on the staff.

8. All note-heads except grace and cue notes (which are smaller) should be the same size, regardless of the position in a space or on a line.

9. A diamond-shaped note-head is used to show the point on a string which is used to produce harmonics on stringed instruments. (*See* page 68.)

10. In the case of chords, notes should be lined up vertically. In the case of the interval of a second, the upper note of the second is on the right of the stem, regardless of the direction of the stem. (*See* STEMS, page 11.)

11. A "cluster." (*See* "Clusters," page 96.)

12. An optional note may appear in a parenthesis.

C. STEMS

1. A stem should be in contact with a note-head.

2. A stem is a thin line.

3. Direction of stems:

   a. The general rule is that stems go in the direction of the most room. When there are more notes on the bottom of a chord, the stem goes up. When there are more on the top, the stem goes down.

b. A stem of a single note below the third line of the staff is on the right side of the note-head and is directed upward; the stem of a note above the third line is on the left side of the note-head and extends downward. Exceptions are as follows:

   • a note which is in a separate voice (notes in the same voice have stems pointing in the same direction).

   • a note which is part of a chord in which most of the notes are on the opposite side of the staff's middle line.

   • a note which is attached to the same beam as other notes but which is not on the same side of the middle line as the majority of notes.

c. In the case of a chord which includes an interval of a second, the higher note of the second is always on the right of the stem, regardless of the stem's direction. When the stem is down, most of the notes are on the right side (including the upper note of the second, since that note is always on the right). When the stem is up, most of the notes are on the left (not including the second). When two notes of the interval of a second are played simultaneously and are in separate voices, the stem of the note of the higher voice points up and that of the lower voice points down. The position of the notes are reversed unless the voices cross over.

4. Length:

   a. The length of a stem for a single note is generally one octave.

   b. A stem is longer when there are several notes on it, usually about three spaces between the note and the end of the stem.

   c. There is often the need to attach stems of different lengths to a beam.

d. In the case of ledger lines, the stem goes from the note-heads to the middle line when the note nearest the staff is anywhere more distant than the first ledger line.

e. The stem of a flat should end two and one-half spaces above the bottom of the flat.

5. Stems of eighth notes which are above and below the middle line are usually beamed above or below both notes.

6. Stems of cue notes and grace notes always extend upward. If the staff is very crowded, the cue note may extend downward. Grace notes always have a line drawn through the flag, when single.

7. To make voice-leading clearer, the stems of one voice are written in the opposite direction from stems of another voice. One note-head with a stem going up and one going down is used to indicate a unison, when the two notes have the same time value.

8. The same stem is not used for notes with different values.

9. A "cluster" (*See* Contemporary Music, page 96.) is a chromatic progression of notes played simultaneously. A heavy line (or a stem on each side) is drawn vertically between the lowest and the highest notes.

10. If two different accidentals apply to two adjacent notes on the same line or space, one stem is drawn between the two note-heads and both accidentals are placed before the notes.

Usually the notation would be A-natural and G-sharp.

11. Flags are always on the right side of the stem.

D. RESTS

1. A whole rest is used when there is a complete bar with no notes in it. (This is not true of a whole *note*, which depends on the meter signature.) A whole rest is placed in the middle of the measure. (The wholenote is placed at the beginning of the measure.)

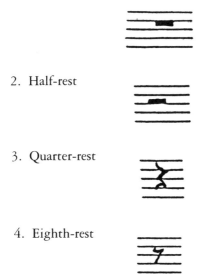

2. Half-rest

3. Quarter-rest

4. Eighth-rest

5. Sixteenth-rests, etc.

6. If a note is in a bar, a whole rest is not used.

7. Rests may last for several bars. The symbol indicating the length of the rest is as follows:

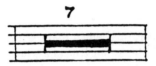

8. The choice of the length of rest depends on the rhythm of the measure. The use of two quarter-rests instead of one half-rest in the following example emphasizes the 3/4 time.

9. When a score has a one-bar rest, it is not necessary to put a "1" over the bar since it is plainly visible. However, it must be used in instrumental parts. A single bar rest has a "1" over it.

10. Each bar may be numbered when there are a few bars of rests.

11. Rests should be written on specific lines whenever possible. However, to avoid crowding, the rests may be moved.

12. When more than one staff is involved in a line of music, rests should be aligned vertically from staff to staff.

13. *See* Cueing (page 64) for special rules concerning rests and cues.

E. ACCIDENTALS

1. Definition: Accidentals are symbols which indicate that a note must be altered or that the alteration is to be cancelled. A key signature at the beginning of a composition includes accidentals of the key in which the music is written. A pitch is altered for one measure by placing the accidental before the note. Some instruments can produce a fraction of a half-tone. (*See* MICROTONES, page 96.)

2. Examples:
flat: the stem ends 2½ spaces above the bottom of the flat. The body fills the space.

sharp: the vertical lines are 2½ spaces long and thin; the horizontal lines are 1 space long and thick.

natural: the sign is 2½ spaces high; the body of it occupies 1 space.

double sharp:

double flat:

3. Position

    a.   In the key signature, the accidentals are close together.

    b.   When an accidental is required between notes, extra room should be left to avoid crowding. One-half space should be left between accidentals and notes.

    c.   When there is more than one accidental before a chord, the accidentals are usually positioned as follows:

    • Accidentals of an octave should be aligned vertically.

    • When there is an interval of a second with each note having its own stem, the order of accidentals is reversed.

This is not true if the voice lines cross over.

- When used to apply to the notes of a trill, there are several ways to write this:

e. When there is to be a key change at the beginning of the next line, this change is shown at the end of the preceding line. This prepares the instrumentalist for the key. An additional device for aiding the player is to use accidental signs in the bar immediately following the key change. Very often double bars are put in before the new key signature. (However, if, as in contemporary music, key changes occur very often, the double bar is not used.)

4. In a tie, accidentals are not written again, except in the case of the tie being carried over to the next line. In that case, the accidental is placed in a parenthesis.

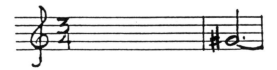

5. Accidentals must be written again when that note is to be played an octave higher or lower.

6. When playing "divisi," accidentals apply to one voice.

7. In the case of a cluster, an accidental is placed above the symbol to indicate the use of only sharps, flats or natural keys. One may also write *"black keys"* or *"white keys."*

F. BEAMS

1. Beams are lines which connect notes, and, by this device, create a grouping.

2. Beams indicate the value of notes, as do flags.

3. Beams follow the ascent or descent of the notes in the group. If the first and the last notes are on the same level, the beam is parallel to the staff lines.

4. Beams occupy one-half the space between the line.

5. Accessory beams are the width of the main beam.

6. Beams are used for grace notes having more than one note. A double beam is used for two notes. A triple beam is used for four or more notes.

7. If all three notes are on one beam in a triplet, the numeral "3" is placed on the side of the beam away from the notes. Room should be left for articulation marks nearer the notes. If the first or last note of a triplet is replaced by a rest, a bracket is used with the "3."
When no beams or flags are called for, brackets are used.

G. FLAGS OR HOOKS

1. The flag is connected to the stem and flares out and then back towards the stem, not quite touching it.

2. With each additional flag, the stem is extended an extra half-space.

H. TIME DOTS
A time dot changes the time value of a note by adding half as much again the time value of the preceding note. The dot is placed in the space after the note-head, or, if the note-head is on a line, on the next higher space.

Two dots may appear in the same space next to each other after the note to show that the value is half the note plus half the dot; that is, the note is held for the value of the note plus half and a quarter of it.

I.   THE CLEF

1. The clef signs are as follows:

   a.   Treble clef (G clef): The end curl encircles the second line from the bottom.

   b.   Bass clef (F clef): The curl at the beginning encircles the fourth line from the bottom. The dots are on either side of this line.

   c.   Movable clefs: The point of a movable clef sign is on a line which is to serve as middle C.

   • Alto or viola clef signs use the middle line as middle C.

• Tenor clef signs use the line which is second from the
top as middle C.

d. Clef for unpitched instruments.

2. Clefs are written close to the front edge unless there is a
change of clef somewhere further along the staff. In the
case of a change during the course of the music the clef sign
is then written just before the bar line of the measure
starting the change, or before the note in the middle of the
bar. The new clef sign is written just before a beat, either
before the note (if the note is on the beat), or before a rest
which is on the beat.

3. Movable clefs are used to avoid too many ledger lines.

4. "8va" indicates that the note is to be played an octave
higher than written. "8va" is the abbreviation for "ottava."
"15ma" indicates that the note is to be played two octaves
higher than written. "15ma" is the abbreviation for "quin-
dicesima." "8" or "15." may be used instead of "8va" or
"15ma." These abbreviations are written above the first
note affected. A broken line is ended by a short vertical
line to the note ending the use of "8," etc. "Loco" is

written at the ending, when the intention is unclear, to show that the passage affected is no longer to be raised. Under the staff, "8va" means that the music is to be played one octave lower than written until the end of the broken line. "Bassa" may be added ("8va bassa"). "Col 8va ^{ba}" means "with ottava bassa."

5. When a clef change occurs at the beginning of a new line, this is indicated at the end of the preceding one.

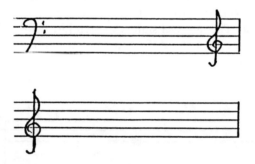

6. Clefs do not change the key.

J. THE STAFF

1. Each staff has five lines, evenly spaced. However, a single line or lines may be added above, below or between staves for unpitched instruments.

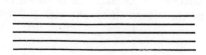

2. Ledger lines have the same spacing as the lines of the staff.

3. If there is only one staff needed at one time for an instrument, there is no vertical line on the left edge of the staff.

4. Manuscript paper has from eight to twenty-four staves.

5. Separate, shared and multiple staves

   a. In a score each instrumental part may have a staff.

   b. Similar instruments may share a staff.

   c. There are usually two wind instruments per staff.

   d. Strings with divisi parts share a staff unless too much difference in parts prove confusing.

   e. Solo parts are placed on separate staves above the others.

   f. Double staves may be required in the case of an instrument requiring two hands, each playing independently. (A piano or a harp is an example.)

   g. Unpitched percussion instruments may use just one line, or two parts may share one staff, each one being assigned a staff line or space.

   h. More than two staves may be needed if a group of the same instruments are divided into several groups, each playing a different part.

   i. Three staves are needed for the organ to show the double staff for the hands and the staff for the foot pedals.

6. A staff may be left blank to show the division of choirs of instruments. A blank staff may also show that a page is

divided; the music may progress from the top half of the page to the bottom half instead of to the next page.

7. When the same notes are to be played by two sets of similar instruments, the second staff may use the term "col primo" ("with the first") to avoid writing the same notes twice.

K. THE BAR LINE

1. Single bar lines are thin, but heavier than those used for stems.

2. Bar lines may extend down a page to group instruments and divided parts in a score. This is not done with vocal parts because of the inclusion of the text.

3. Double lines

   a. Double bar lines having two thin lines are used to mark a change in the key signature or meter signature. If the changes occur very frequently, as they do in much contemporary music, the double bar line is not used.

   b. A set of double bar lines, having one thick and one thin line is used to designate the boundaries of a section; the thick line is the outer boundary.

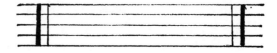

L. BRACES AND BRACKETS

> 1. A horizontal bracket is used with triplets, etc., in certain
>   cases. (See METER, page 35.)
>
> 2. A vertical brace is used with a thin line on the left side
>   joining two staves for two-staved music (as in the case of
>   keyboard instruments).

> 3. A thin line and a heavy bracket are drawn vertically to-
>   gether to join all staves of a score or of a choir of instru-
>   ments. An additional bracket may join groups of similar
>   instruments; e.g., all the woodwinds. This added bracket
>   or a brace may join staves of a divided group of instru-
>   ments; e.g., two groups of violins.

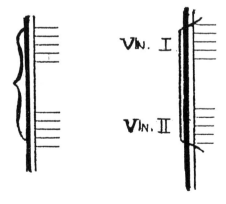

M. REPETITIONS AND TREMOLOS

1. Notes that are to be repeated are so indicated by a line or lines (slashes) through the end of the stems or through the imagined stems of whole notes. The slashes represent the time value of the notes and, therefore, the number of times the notes are to be played. These lines are at an angle to the stem.

2. If there is no stem, the slashes are at the same angle as if there were a stem.

3. A tremolo consists of two pitches alternating. When the pitch of a note is made to waver (as in the case of stringed instruments), the slashes are placed through the stem away from the note-head, or, if there are no stems, through the imagined stems. When two definite pitches are to be alternated, the slashes appear between the stems, parallel to the imagined beam or between the imagined stems of whole notes.

   a. Measured tremolos have a specific number of repetitions per beat. The number of beams represents the value of the group of notes. Two notes are equal to the value of one. The first figure can be notated in full.

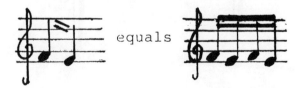

b. *Unmeasured tremolos* are those that have no specific number of repetitions. If the tremolo is between two notes, two slashes are drawn parallel to the beam and between the stems or imagined stems of whole notes, following the direction of the first note to the second. It is advisable to write the term "trem." above ("non trem." ends it). "Trem." written in indicates that this is not a measured tremolo even though there are three beams.

c. The *trill* is unmeasured. When using an auxiliary note, a grace note is written before the trill. It is best to indicate which notes are used in the trill.

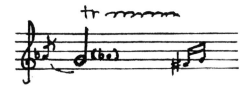

4. Repeated figures within a bar may be represented by slashes after the first notated presentation. One slash indicates eighth-notes, two indicate sixteenths, etc.

5. To repeat a bar, the numeral "1" is placed above the first fully-notated bar to be repeated. A repeat sign appears in the middle of the bar which repeats, each bar having successive numerals above and centered over the bar. Actually, the numerals are used when there are more than two repeats.

CONCORDIA COLLEGE LIBRARY
BRONXVILLE, N. Y. 10708

6. A double repeat is one in which two successive bars are immediately repeated.

7. In the case of repeats involving a double staff as in keyboard music, the repeat sign is drawn between the two staves.

8. The repetition of a section is indicated by two bar lines (a heavy and a thin bar line) close together at the beginning of the section and at the end. The heavy lines are the outside boundaries. The dots are placed after the first double bar lines on either side of the middle staff line and before the double bar lines at the end of the section. The first double bar lines are not placed at the beginning of the work.

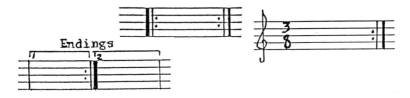

9. *Da Capo* (*D.C.*) means "from the head." This indicates that one is to return to the beginning and repeat the section. *D.C.* is placed under the staff. *Fine*, written under the staff, is used to indicate the point at which the composition is ended.

10. *Dal Segno* (*D.S.*) means "from the sign." This indicates that one is to return to the sign,

𝄋. or **𝄋.**

(which appears both above the staff; and below and above the double staff). The music is to be repeated until the new sign ✛ (which is placed above the staff, and below and above the double staff) or until the end is reached.

11. "D.C. al ✛ " or "D.S. al ✛ " means to return to the beginning or to the sign 𝄋. and proceed to the new sign ✛ and then to the coda.

12. Repeat symbols indicating a repeated bar are not placed at the beginning of a page, since the first fully notated bar cannot easily be seen and referred to.

N. CUE AND GRACE NOTES

1. Cue notes and grace notes have small note-heads.

2. A grace note always has the stem up with a flag. The flag has a line through it. Beams are used for grace notes having more than one note.
A double beam is used for a two-note group; a triple beam for four or more notes.

3. The stems of cue notes point upward, unless the staff is very crowded.

4. In the case of cue notes, articulation marks, such as slurs, are reversed to make the staff less cluttered. Since the stems are up, these marks are written over the stems.

O. THE KEY SIGNATURE

1. The key signature is written before the meter signature.

2. When the key changes, the old key signature is not carried to the next line.

3. When changing keys, a double bar line is drawn, then old accidentals are sometimes nullified and followed by new ones. In the first bar following, the new accidentals may be indicated for clarity.

4. When the key change is at the beginning of a line, this is anticipated by writing the change at the end of the preceding line. No bar line is drawn at the end of this line.

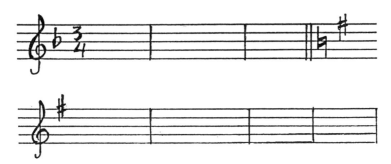

P. TIME OR METER

1. The meter signature is placed after the key signature, or after the clef, if there is no key signature. It fits between the top and the bottom lines of the staff.

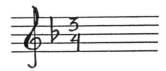

2. The meter signature does not appear on the staff following the first one unless the signature changes.

3. A double bar line is placed before the new meter signature.

4. When the meter signature changes often, as in the case of contemporary music, a single bar line is drawn before the new meter signature.

5. When the meter signature changes at the beginning of the line, this must be indicated at the end of the preceding line.

(Sometimes called "common time")

6. **C** means $\frac{4}{4}$ time. (Sometimes called "common time")

   ¢ means $\frac{2}{2}$ time. (Sometimes called "cut time")

7. When the meter signature is unusual, such as $\frac{5}{4}$, for the sake of clarity, dots may be used to divide the bar. Confusing them with time dots is avoided by ample spacing.

8. A cadenza is an unmeasured flowing passage. There are no bar lines.

9. When there are extra notes in a group which legitimately should have fewer, it is so indicated by the number of notes, a colon and the legitimate number of notes.

10. Pauses (Fermata, Grand Pause and Vuota). (See TEMPO, page 42.)

11. A triplet or another similar grouping of notes which has extra notes and which is to be played in the same amount of time as the legitimate number of notes must be handled in the following ways:

    a. Extra space should be left between groups.

    b. In dealing with groups of eighth-notes, sixteenths, etc., a beam is drawn to connect the stems, unless there is a rest in place of the first or last note. (In this case a bracket is used. See page 35.)

c. A bracket is drawn (usually outside the staff, to avoid cluttering)

• when the first or last note is not played.

• when there are notes of different values involved.

• when the note stems are in the opposite direction or in both directions. It is placed over or under the staff, depending on the amount of crowding in the staff.

• when there is a large number of notes involved.

• when the group is made up of quarter-notes, etc. (notes that do not require flags or beams).

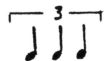

d. When there is a series of groups each having the same number of notes with the same value, the numeral is written for the first group and is understood for the succeeding ones.

e. In compound time these groupings may be written in two ways.

Q. THE SLUR (The tie, the legato slur and the phrase mark)

1. The tie symbol (a curved line under or over two or more notes) is a slur between two identically pitched notes and signifies holding the first note for the time value of the two. When more than two notes are tied, the slur mark must be drawn from one note-head to the next.

2. The legato slur indicates that the notes involved are to be played smoothly. Therefore, in the case of the strings, one stroke of the bow would be used; in the case of the voice, one breath would be used.

3. The phrase mark and the legato slur should be outside the staff, if there is not too much crowding. If most of the note-heads are above, the slur must be above them. If they are mostly below, the curve is below. (In the case of cue notes, articulation marks are usually over the stems.)

4. The *phrase mark* extends to the end of a tie or slur. The *slur* is not to touch the note-head.

5. In a *tie*, accidentals are not written before the second note, unless it is carried to the next line, in which case it is put in parentheses.

6. *Ties* are divided between two chords in the following ways:

   a. in order to give a balanced appearance, the curves are divided, those above curving up and those below curving down.

b. in the case of an interval of a second that is tied, the curves must go in opposite directions.

7. The slur is outside the accent, which is outside marks such as those for staccato. The tie is closest to the notes. A staccato dot under a slur is a "portato" dot.

R. DYNAMICS, EXPRESSION AND ARTICULATION

1. Directions for dynamics are written below the staff or between two staves joined by a brace (as in piano music). They are placed above the staff in vocal music so as not to interfere with the text. The symbol (f , for example) is placed on a vertical line with the first note involved. Small letters are used.

2. After a period of rest the dynamics must be indicated.

3. In the score, dynamics are shown under every part.

4. The symbols for the dynamics are written on a slant.

$$pp$$

5. Commonly used symbols:

a. pp (*pianissimo*) = very soft.

b. p (*piano*) = soft.

c. 𝑚𝑝 (*mezzo piano*) = moderately soft.

d. 𝑚 (*moderato*) = in a moderate way.

e. 𝑚𝑓 (*mezzo forte*) = moderately loud.

f. 𝑓 (*forte*) = loud.

g. 𝑓𝑓 (*fortissimo*) = very loud.

h. ⟨ (*crescendo*) = becoming loud. The abbreviation "*cresc.*" may be used instead.

i. ⟩ (*decrescendo*) (*diminuendo*) = becoming softer. The abbreviation "*decresc.*" or "*dim.*" may be used instead.

j. 𝑠𝑓 (*sforzando*) = heavily accented.

k. 𝑓𝑝 (*forte-piano*) = loud, then soft.

l. (*legato*) = progressing from note to note in the smoothest possible way.

m. (*portamento*) = sounding one note after the other in the smoothest way.

n. (*détaché*) = gently, detached from each other.

o. (*marcato*) = heavily accented.

p. (*tenuto*) = sustained.

q. = accented strongly. The size of the accent mark is about the width of one staff space.

r. (*portato*) = half-staccato.

s. (*staccato*) = a short note; that is, released at once.

t. (*staccato*) = a very accented staccato.

u. Pauses (See TEMPO, page 42.)

⌢• (*fermata*)

⌐•⌐ (*long fermata*)

G. P. (*Grand Pause*)

vuota (*void*)

v. Pedals for the piano

⁃ ⌐ means that the damper pedal is depressed and released.

⁃ 〜〜 means that the damper pedal is to be depressed and released alternately at appropriate points in the music.

⁃ *Ped.* means that the damper pedal is to be depressed.

⁃ (*) indicates the release of the damper pedal.

⁃ *U.C.* (*Una Corda*) calls for the use of the left or the soft pedal.

⁃ *T.C.* (*Tre Corde*) means that the left or soft pedal is to be released.

⁃ *S.P.* (*sustaining pedal*) calls for the middle pedal to be down as long as the horizontal bracket indicates.

w. The pedalling indication for the harp to change pitches is placed at the point of change but in the most visible place. (See HARP, page 78.)

Symbols for the use of the heel and the toe when pedalling the organ:

U = heel

∧ = toe

S. TEMPO

1. At the beginning of a piece of music the tempo direction is positioned above the key signature. The first word is capitalized. The word used to describe the tempo is often followed by the metronome marking; e.g., Allegro ♩ = ca 104. "Ca" is the abbreviation for "circa" which means "about." This marking means that there are about 104 quarter-notes to a minute.

2. Changes of tempo are written above the staff throughout the music. The first letter is not capitalized, except at the beginning.

3. Suggested terms for degrees of tempo:

   a. *Largo* = slowly, broadly, expressively.

   b. *Grave* = slowly and seriously, with dignity.

   c. *Adagio* = slowly.

   d. *Andante* = slowly, but moving along.

   e. *Andante* = less slowly.

   f. *Allegretto* = faster, but not as fast as "Allegro."

   g. *Allegro* = fast and bright.

   h. *Accelerando* = becoming faster.

   i. *Presto* = very fast.

   j. *Ritardando* ("Rit") = slowing down gradually.

   k. *Ritenuto* = immediate holding back and slowing.

   l. *Rubato* = giving more or less time to notes in order to be expressive, but not altering the length of time of the phrase so that the phrase fits into the tempo of the composition.

   m. *Colla Parta* = a term for each instrumental part which indicates that the player must follow the conductor's rubato. This term is written in each part under the staff with a fermata.

   n. *A tempo* = back to the original tempo.

4. A few modifiers:

   a. *Più* = more.

   b. *Meno* = less.

   c. *Molto* = very.

   d. *-issimo* = very (example "Prestissimo")

5. Pauses

   a. The Fermata ⌢ indicates that a note or rest is
       extended past the value of the note. The arch is high.
       ⌐·¬ may be used for a longer pause. These symbols
       appear over the staff and, if there is another voice on
       the same staff, an additional one should appear upside
       down under the staff.

   b. The "Grand Pause" ("G.P.") written under the staff is
       used when there is no sound from anyone, solo or
       orchestra. This must be written in all the instrumental
       parts, but it is not needed in the score. "G.P. in
       tempo" is the term for strict rhythm. "G.P." with a
       fermata indicates a pause that is longer than the
       rhythm that is called for in strict rhythm.

   c. *Vuota*, meaning "void," describes the fact that the
       orchestra is silent but that someone is performing. The
       term is written under the staff in each part.

   d. *Luftpause* is a short pause for breath. ⁊

T. SYMBOLS FOR EMBELLISHMENTS AND ORNAMENTS
    are positioned above the staff.

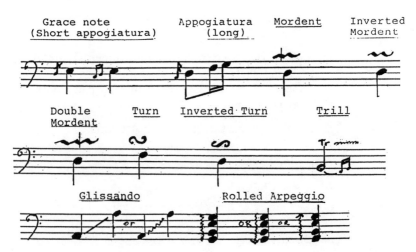

U. CHORDS

1. A chord must have the notes exactly on a vertical line with each other on one side of the stem with the seconds aligned on the other side, unless the chord is broken. Each note must be the same size as the others. (Sometimes, in the case of a very thick texture, small notes are used to highlight a strand.)

2. The rolled arpeggio uses the sign ξ before the chord. (See above.)

3. A broken chord is written showing the exact time value of each note, since the value of each note may be different.

4. In order to position a chord of whole notes which include seconds, the stem must be imagined.

V. INDICATIONS OF DIVISION

1. *div.* (divisi) means the separation of parts where one would expect one voice; for example, the first violins would divide into more than one section and each play a different part (written on a separate staff or using separate stems). One vertical line connects these staves. When dealing with woodwinds and brass which may be divided into groups, each part has a separate staff or page until joining again (*a 2*, *a 3*, etc., or *unis.*).

2. *div. a 3* may be written with two staves (two voices being on one staff) or with three staves.

3. *div. a 4* or multiples of two may have two parts on each staff.

4. *non-div.* means that the instruments are to play together.

5. *unis.* (unison) ends the division.

6. *a 2* means that the two groups of instruments are to play the same notes together. Roman numeral *I* means the same thing after div. *a 2* is placed above the staff. Instead of using *a 2*, stems in opposite directions may be used, usually when the unison passage is short. Scores do not have two staves for *a 2*, but parts do.

7. *Tutti* means that all the instruments are playing.

8. *Solo* indicates that one instrument is playing the part.

9. *Gli altri* is the term used to explain that the rest of the instruments are to play; e.g., the rest of the violins are to join in.

10. *Tacet* at the beginning of the composition, placed in a part under the first tempo indication, means that the instrument does not play until later; e.g., *tacet to bar 199. Tacet al fine* indicates that the instrument does not play anymore in that piece of music.

W. PEDAL MARKS are to be written in to indicate the use of the foot to activate an instrument. (See DYNAMICS, EXPRESSION AND ARTICULATION, page 40.)

1. *For piano performance*
The damper pedal on the right is the pedal usually indicated, although much of the decision is the performer's. The marks appear below the double staff. The term *Ped.* is the abbreviation used for depressing the pedal; an asterisk (*) indicates the release. The use of the *soft pedal* on the left is also indicated below the double staff by the abbreviation *U.C.* (una corda). *T.C.* (tre corde) is used to release the pedal. The use of the *sustaining pedal* in the middle is shown by the abbreviation *S.P.* (sustaining pedal) under the double staff. A horizontal bracket is placed under the whole passage. The *damper pedal* marks appear below the other pedal signs.

2. *For harp performance* (See INSTRUMENTS: Instruments using more than one staff, page 77.)
   The pedals are used for the pitch setting of the strings. A group of letters or a diagram is placed above or between or under the staves at the beginning of the music. Changes during the music are written at the point of change in the most visible place.

3. *For organ performance*
   Pedals are used for the production of bass tones. The symbols **U** (use heel) and **∧** (use toe) may appear under (for the left foot) and over (for the right foot) the lowest staff. These symbols are useful for the student.

X. BAR NUMBERS OR LETTERS (See GENERAL PREPARATION, page 50.)

PART III: GENERAL PREPARATION

A. CLARITY is the most important point to emphasize.

    1. There must not be any crowding.

    2. Spacings should reflect time values; e.g., a little extra space between groups of triplets.

    3. The divisions of the measure must be clear.

    4. Measures must not be broken at the end of a line.

    5. For the sake of clarity, symbols indicating a repeated bar cannot be used at the beginning of a page. The bar must be written out.

    6. In score writing, it is crucial to have all parts in perfect alignment.

    7. Ledger lines have the same spacing as the lines on the staff. It is sometimes necessary to proceed to another clef to avoid many ledger lines.

    8. It is helpful, if at all possible, for the right-hand page of a manuscript to end with a rest so that there is enough time for the performer to turn the page. This is extremely important.

9. If there are three or more bars to be repeated or not to be played (full measure rests), the bars must be numbered. Numbering helps the performer.

10. Note-heads and stems must be of the proper length and size; directions properly placed.

B. INSTRUMENTATION

1. On the page before the first page of music there should be a list called *"Instrumentation"* followed by the information about transposition. (It shall be stated that it is a concert score or a transposed score.) (See THE TRANSPOSING INSTRUMENTS, page 49.)

   The order of listing the instruments is generally as follows:

> Piccolos
> Flutes
> Oboes
> English Horns
> Clarinets
> Bassoons
>
> Horns
> Trumpets
> Trombones
> Tubas
> Timpani
> Other percussion
>
> Extra instruments (such as harp,
> piano, organ and celesta) and
> choral parts
>
> Violins
> Violas
> Violoncellos
> Double basses

The name of the solo instrument is generally above the string section.

a. On the first page and on each succeeding page of orchestral scores instruments are listed in a vertical line on the left side of the staves. The order is as follows:

Woodwinds
Brass
Percussion
Extra instruments and choral parts
Solo
Strings

b. Each name should be written out in full on the first page of the movement or section.

c. Groups of instruments are separated by a staff, if possible.

d. If there are more staves than instruments, a staff may be skipped to clarify the grouping. When the page is divided because there are only enough instruments to use part of the staves at a time, two diagonal lines are drawn under an empty staff to show the separation of the page.

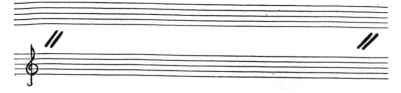

e. A single line may be used for unpitched instruments. (See page 73.)

f. Scores do not show divided parts by using two staves. Instrumental parts, however, may use different staves for *divisi*.

g. A change back to one staff from two staves does not occur until the start of a new line.

2. The transposing instruments.

a. There are two kinds of scores:

• In the concert score (C score) all notation is equal to actual pitches sounded. In the score all instrumental parts are in the same key as the C instruments. (The parts must then be transposed by the instrumentalists of the transposing instruments.) The concert score is used a great deal in twentieth century music.

- A transposed score is used traditionally. In this type of score the transposing instrument's part is written in the key of the instrument, just as it would be on the separate part of the instrumentalist. (When C is written for the B-flat clarinet, B-flat is sounded.) The notation for transposing instruments is equal to pitches at an interval above or below the actual pitches sounded, the distance being that which separates the instrument's key from C.

   b. In writing a part for transposing instruments, those instruments with a pitch below the C instruments will compensate by transposing to a pitch above that of the C instruments. Those above are transposed below. For example, the part for the horn in F (pitched a fifth below C) is written a fifth above.

C. THE BEGINNING OF THE WORK

1. If there is only one staff, there is no vertical line along the left edge. Otherwise, a vertical line connects all the staves of one line of music.

2. A vertical brace and a line is drawn on the left edge if one instrument is using two staves; e.g., the piano.

3. A vertical bracket is drawn for a choir of similar instruments.

4. The clef is the closest symbol to the left edge on each line.

5. The key signature is written before the meter signature.

6. A brace outside the bracket and line may show that there are two groups of the same instruments; e.g., Violins I and Violins II.

D. LOCATION OF DIRECTIONS

1. Directions for tempi are written above the staff.

2. Directions for dynamics are written below the staff or between a double staff, with the exception of vocal music because of the text.

3. Directions for alternating instruments (flute to oboe, for example) are placed above the staff just before the change of key if a second instrument is to be a transposing instrument.

E. BAR NUMBERS (OR LETTERS)
Three types of numbering are needed for measures:

1. A multiple bar rest sign is advisable when there are more than three bars of rest.

In the case of many bars of repetitions, the bar with the material to be repeated is fully notated and counted as number 1. Each numeral is positioned above and in the center of the measure. It is placed between the staves in a double staff.

2. Rehearsal numbers are used no less frequently than every ten measures; they are also placed at the beginning of difficult, confusing or important places in the music. A letter may be used but there are many numbers and only a

limited supply of letters. The number is enclosed in a square. It is placed over the beginning of the bar. The more numbers used, the more the cost of the printing, but clarity is essential. Rehearsal numbers contribute to the success of rehearsals. The score's rehearsal numbers should be shown on every individual part.

3. Simple numbering of the measure from the beginning of the composition is handled by placing a numeral in a parenthesis above the staff on the left of center.

F. REPETITIONS AND RESTS. (See NOTATION, pages 28–31 and 15–17.)

G. FORMATS FOR TRADITIONAL MUSIC

1. General information

   a. A suggested succession of pages:

      • Cover

      • Inside cover which may be blank.

      • The first page on the right which is the title page. This should include the name of the composer, the title (with the key and opus number), the editor and the publisher (including his address). Copyright information may appear on this page.

- The back of the first page which may be blank or contain the table of contents. The instrumentation list may be on this page.

- The second page on the right which will have the first page of music.

b. Turning the page.

    - The turn must be taken at the end of the odd pages on the right unless there are only two pages; in this case, the first page may be on the left.

    - If the first page has no rest at the end of the last measure, page two (on the left) may be the first page of music. Page one is then blank.

    - "V.S." ("turn quickly") may be written at the end of the page to indicate that an empty space appears at the end of this page, but that notes follow immediately at the top of the next page.

    - "*Time*" can be written on the bottom of a completely filled page if the next page starts with a rest.

c. If there are only a few pages, they may be attached side by side or in accordion style and opened flat on the music stand.

d. Solo parts

    - The name of the instrument appears over the first staff in the left corner.

    - The title is written above and in the center of the second staff.

    - The number of the movement, act, etc. is placed on and in the center of the second staff. A Roman numeral is used.

    - The composer's name is placed directly over the right side of the second staff.

    - The music starts on the third staff.

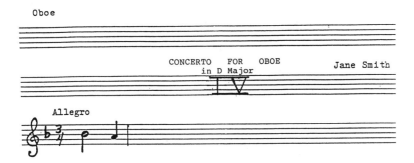

e. The suggested number of staves on a page (also see page 3):

- In music for the piano and voice: twelve-staved paper (multiples of three).

- In opera vocal scores: fourteen-staved paper.

- For orchestral scores: thirty (plus)-staved paper.

- In vocal and orchestral scores: twelve- or more staved paper.

2. Full symphony orchestra scores.
   The full score and parts follow the guidelines set forth previously under GENERAL PREPARATION. (The name "score" is derived from the fact that a line scores through the staves.) See the example on page 54.

3. Theater orchestra scores.
   The difference between these and symphony orchestra scores is that the piano part appears on the bottom. (In symphony orchestra scores it appears above the strings.) The saxophone parts are placed under the woodwinds.

4. Band scores.
   Bands do not include the string section. The layout is the same as previously described. Since many instruments are needed, sharing staves when practical will cut down on the size of the paper required.

Example: the beginning
     of a typical score

a. The symphonic or "concert" band is made up of brass, woodwinds and percussion instruments. It is concerned with music itself rather than augmenting another activity, such as athletic games. Listing of instruments approximately follows that of the symphony orchestra score. However, in the case of the "concert" band score, the order is more flexible and often has the piano and harp parts written at the bottom, if they are included.

b. The brass band usually has about twenty-five brass instruments, including cornets, flugelhorns, horns, euphoniums, trombones and tubas. Marching band instrumentalists use smaller sized paper so that they can clip it on to the instruments as they march. (See PAPER, page 3.)

5. Chamber music scores.

a. In music for two like instruments playing a duo, the two staves may be joined by a brace. If the instruments are not similar, a bracket is used.

b. In a brass ensemble, the order of instruments is as follows:

   Trumpets
   Horns
   Trombones
   Euphoniums
   Tubas

   A bracket must join all the staves, and bar lines extend through all the staves.

c. In a string ensemble, the order of instruments is the same as the string section in an orchestral score. As in the case of the brass ensemble, the bracket on the left and the bar lines join all the staves.

d. In a woodwind ensemble, the order of instruments in the score is the same as that of the woodwind section in an orchestral score. However, when a horn is included in a quintet, the horn is placed above the bassoon, since the bassoon employs the bass clef. A bracket joins all the staves and the bar lines extend through all the staves.

e. When the piano is part of the small ensemble of like instruments, the double staff is below the staves of the instrumental parts. This is true of the small ensemble of unlike instruments. But in a score for a large mixed ensemble, the order of the instruments is the same as in an orchestral score; the piano part is placed above the strings. A brace joins the staves of the piano part. Bar lines go through all the staves of like instruments but do not connect with the piano staves. A bracket on the left connects instruments of a choir in mixed ensembles.

f. Duos, trios, quartets, quintets, etc., of like instruments use brackets and bar lines through all the staves. In all cases, tempo directions are above the top staff and dynamic directions are under each staff and between the two piano staves. (Mixed ensemble scores list instruments in the same order as orchestral scores.) Sometimes staves with treble clef signs are above those with bass clef signs. Occasionally the percussion is placed at the bottom of the score.

When several instruments from each choir are involved in a large ensemble, the choirs are bracketed and one bar line is drawn at the beginning through all the choirs. After the beginning the bar line extends only through the staves of each choir. See the example on page 57.

g. Percussion ensemble scores.
Each instrument has an individual line: first, those using the treble clefs, then bass clefs, then the timpani. This is not so in mixed ensemble scores; these usually have the timpani alone above the others, then the instruments using the treble clef grouped together, then those using the bass clef, followed by the instruments that are unpitched.

6. Concerto scores.
In orchestral concerto scores the solo part appears above the

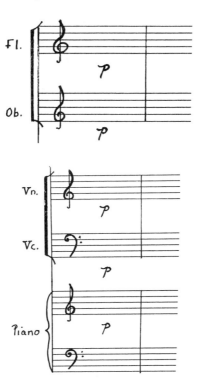

strings, but this does not occur in band scores. In the latter case the solo part is placed above the brass.

7. Music for solo instruments with piano accompaniment.

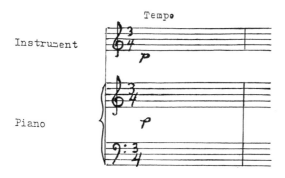

Note the bar lines and the brace.

8. Organ music has two staves joined together by a brace for the manuals, as well as a staff under these for the pedals. The bar lines connect the two staves for the manuals but not the pedal staff.

9. Two-staved music (as for solo piano, harp and celesta) has the brace joining the two staves. The bar lines join the staves as well.

10. Music for two pianos has four staves.

11. Music for duets (one piano).
    The arrangement may be the same as in the case of two pianos (preferable since each player can see both parts) or, as is usually done, with one part appearing on the left pages and the other on the right pages. In the latter case, obviously, the turn must be at the same time for both.

12. Vocal music.

    a. Choral music.

       • The order of vocal parts are as follows:

         — Soprano
           Alto
           Tenor
           Bass

       • The piano part is on the bottom of the other parts. Each part has its own staff. A bracket joins the vocal parts; one vertical line joins the vocal and the instrumental part. The bar lines are not drawn through more than one staff because of printed lyrics. Indications for dynamics as well as for tempi are placed above each vocal part. The name of the writer of the text must be printed over the first tempo direction. Credits are on the bottom of the page and centered. When there is a solo part, it appears on the top staff. (See p. 60).

    b. The vocal part with a small group of instruments of the same choir is placed on the top staff.

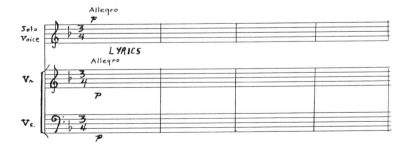

Copyright information

c. The vocal part with a larger mixed ensemble with strings is usually placed above the strings; if there are no strings, above the brass. A bracket groups each choir. Bar lines go through the staves of a choir of instrumental parts but not through the vocal part. (See p. 61.)

d. Solo songs
Special paper having an extra space between the vocal part and the piano part can be obtained. This space is used for the lyrics.

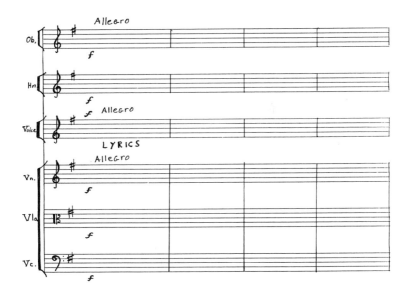

e. At the beginning of the lines, bar lines connect the three staves. A brace joins the two piano staves. Bar lines for each measure do not connect vocal and piano parts because of the lyrics.

f. Opera scores.

An example:

From DIE MEISTERSINGER von NÜRNBERG by Richard Wagner

H. TIPS

1. When a mistake is made on translucent paper, it may be cut out with a razor blade against a ruler. To replace it, a space is left between the edges of the insert and the original paper so that a dark line will not appear when it is printed. It is attached with Scotch Tape #810.

2. The last staff may be cut off when there is a mistake. It will simply appear blank in the printed copy. However, care must be taken to avoid losing the smaller page.

3. Sections to be repeated can be duplicated by printing. However, care must be taken to indicate the proper rehearsal numbers.

4. Turns of pages must be done at the end of the odd pages. Therefore, odd pages are on the right.

5. If there is more than one page, no fewer than eight staves are needed on a page.

PART IV: CUEING

A. CUEING is a method of helping a performer enter the music correctly after having a specific number of bars of rests. In an instrumental part the notes of another instrument which is playing during this rest period are written with notation peculiar to cueing. Cueing is particularly important when there has not been enough rehearsal time.

B. BASIC RULES.

   1. The name of the cueing instrument must appear over the staff at the beginning of the cueing.

   2. The note-heads of cue notes are small.

   3. The stems usually point upward, although this is occasionally impractical.

   4. A full-sized whole rest is placed beneath or above the notes being played to show that the original instrument is resting.

   5. The cue notes of the cueing instrument are transposed into the key of the instrument to be cued, if the keys are not the same.

The difference in pitch between the transposing instrument which is cueing and the instrument which is being

64

cued is treated by compensating. An example would be that of the B-flat clarinet cueing a violin. Since the B-flat clarinet has a C which sounds one whole step lower, in order for the violins to hear the required pitch (C), music of the clarinet must be transposed one whole step higher than that of the violin. Therefore, to hear the same C, the clarinet plays a D. However, the cue note in the C instrument part would be written *C* so that the violinist would not have to transpose as he reads it. If the clef is different, it is helpful to change to the clef of the instrument to be cued.

6. Cueing is used when there are more than ten bars rest. There is a phrase of cueing immediately. Rests may then occur when there is no need to cue, but there must be another phrase of cue notes before the original instrument reenters. An example of good cueing in twenty-four bars of rest would be eight bars of cue notes, eight bars of rest and eight bars of cueing (unless the cueing phrase is longer or shorter or unless there is something important happening as suggested in the next rule).

7. Cues occur at every change of

   a. tempo
   b. meter
   c. key

8. Cues must be treated carefully.

   a. No chords are needed, just single notes.

   b. Articulation, expression and dynamic indications should be included.

9. A cueing passage must appear no less often than once in every thirty bars of rest.

10. The phrase chosen to cue an instrument should have some special character or motion.

11. There is no rest necessary under the staff if there is a whole rest in the cueing.

12. A line between staves may be used for cues by unpitched percussion.

13. Cue notes must be uncrowded.

14. When using *"aleatory"* material for cueing, it is sufficient to write in "aleatory passage." This means that at that point the performance is left up to the performer, mathematical laws of chance decided upon by the composer, abstract design, etc.

C. TIPS.

1. Complicated compositions must have more cues.

2. An instrument with a dominant sound, such as the piccolo or trumpet is good for cueing. The voice is difficult to hear, especially from the orchestra pit during an opera. In addition, words are easily changed just before a performance and, therefore, cannot be relied upon.

   Instruments that are near other instruments and are, therefore, heard easily may be used for cueing. Instruments of similar range are also often used for cueing.

PART V: INSTRUMENTS

A. STRINGS

    1. The clefs ordinarily used by each group of instruments are as follows:

        a. Violins—treble (G) clef.

        b. Violas—alto (C) clef or treble (G) clef.

        c. Cellos—usually the bass (F) clef, often the tenor clef or treble (G) clef.

        d. Bass—bass (F) clef and tenor or treble clef for harmonics.

    2. If the violins are divided, each section needs its own staff. If the solo violin and the violins I have the same notes, their parts may be on the same staff.

    3. The strings are numbered. I (the first string) has the highest pitch.

    4. Fingering may be written above the note. However, room must be allowed for other performance marks between the note-head and the numeral for fingering.

67

5. When using harmonics, notes may be written at pitch. (A small circle over the note means that it is a natural harmonic.  The instrumentalist will produce the desired pitch. If the composer wants a special effect, he must indicate this. This is the simplest method. However, it also can be written in a more directive way, which is especially useful when employing artificial harmonics. The top note in parenthesis is the actual pitch. The lowest note (two octaves below the pitch desired) represents the point pressed firmly. The diamond-shaped note (never filled in) represents the point on the string which is pressed lightly.

6. A small circle is placed above the note to show that it is an open string. This is a larger and flatter circle than that for a natural harmonic.

7. The tremolo (See Page 28) is indicated by slashes on an angle to the stem.

8. Bowing must be shown.

   a. A slur indicates the use of one bow stroke for more than one note. This slur is outside other kinds of slurs.

   b. Plain bowing symbols which appear above the notes on the instrumental parts.

   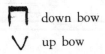 down bow

   up bow

   c. Other commonly used bowings

      • *Détaché* indicates the use of large, vigorous bowing strokes which are separate.

- *Martelé* means heavy, separate strokes ending abruptly. Sometimes the term itself is written in, alone or with the added instruction of using the frog or point of the bow.

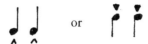

- *Staccato* means short and released quickly. *Group staccato* may be either a few notes played staccato but on one bow, or two repeated notes that are detached from each other by stopping the bow.

- *Louré* (*portato*) means to separate each note of a series of notes taken in a slur. is the way the notes appear. This is used in a slow, singing passage.

- *Spiccato* is the term used to mean a light stroke.

- *Jeté* (*ricochet, saltando, sautillé*) indicates that the bow bounces rapidly.

- Tremolos (See NOTATION; REPETITIONS AND TREMOLOS, pages 28–31.)

- *Pizz.* (*pizzicato*) means "plucked," and *arco*, meaning "bow," signifies the end of pizzicato. This is written above the staff. There are no dots or dashes between *pizz.* and *arco*. "Pizz." remains in effect until "arco," even if there are rests between. When the pizzicato is to vibrate, this notation would be used:

— *Snap pizz.* (a very strong pizzicato) is indicated by the symbol ♧ . *Arco* is used to end it. ♧ is also used in directions for cello indicating the thumb position.

— *Pizz. gliss.* (*pizzicato glissando*) calls for the sound to go up or down.

— *Nail pizzicato* calls for the string to be plucked by the fingernail rather than the soft fingertip. The effect is bright, sharp and metallic. ⊙ or ⊚

— *Ruvido* calls for a rough sound.

— *Arp* (arpeggio) signifies a roll of notes. ⌇ or ⌇ may be used too.

— *Sul pont.* (*sul ponticello*) means "over the bridge." The bow is played very close to or at the bridge of the violin. The effect is a harder and more nasal tone. This is often used with a tremolo.

— *Sul tasto* is the direction which requires the bowing to be slightly over the fingerboard for a softer, flute-like tone ("*flautando*").

— *Punta d'arco* means with "the point of the bow."

— *Col legno* is used to obtain a dry effect. This is produced by striking the strings with the stick of the bow.

— *Ord.* (*modo ordinario*) is used to cancel a special effect and return to the normal way.

9. *L.V.* indicates the fact that the string is to be allowed to vibrate. ![symbol] will stop the vibrating.

10. *Con sord.* (*con sordino*) means "with the mute." *Senza sord.* means "without a mute." The mute gives a quieter and more mysterious effect.

11. The guitar, although a stringed instrument, is not considered part of the classical string section. It is used primarily in current popular and folk music. (See CONTEMPORARY MUSIC; GUITAR, page 113–117.) Classical guitar music employs the notation of other classical and traditional music.

B. BRASS AND WOODWINDS

1. Some players play more than one instrument. An oboist often takes over the English horn. The words *to Eng. Hn.* must be written at the end of the oboe part. Ideally, there are rests while the player changes instruments. When the horn enters, there is a key change to accommodate the horn. *Eng. Hn.* is not written again at this point. A flutist may play the piccolo as well as the flute. (No transposition is necessary since they are both C instruments.)

2. Because of fingering, particularly with respect to the clarinet, ledger lines are used instead of "8va."

3. For notating more than one voice, see pages 14 and 43–44.

4. Tonguing is not usually indicated in the music. But when using the effect of tremolo or "flutter tongue," obtained by rolling the tongue, the words are written above the staff; or three slashes are drawn through the stems.

5. In scores, usually no key signatures are used on the staff for the horn. Therefore, it is important to name the key of the instrument at the beginning.

6. Brass instruments use mutes made of wood or metal. It is important to specify after a period of rest whether or not a mute is to be used. *Con sord.* (con sordino) means "with mute"; *senza sord.* means "without the mute." Very little muting is done by the woodwinds.

7. The horn is usually muted by placing a pear- or cone-shaped piece of metal, wood, or cardboard into the bell, thus allowing some air to escape, not changing the pitch, but altering the timbre. *Con sordino (sord.)* or *with mute* is placed above the staff. *Senza sordino* or *open* cancels the use of the mute.

   The horn is "stopped" when the bell is closed as much as possible with the hand, and lip tension is increased. This raises the pitch one-half tone and has to be transposed down again. The tone quality is changed in this way. A cross above each note indicates the stopping. *Stopped* may be written under the staff. *Cuivré* shows that a brassy effect is desired. " " above the note is used to show that it is an open note. Often *bouché-cuivré* is written to show that the note is to be stopped and brassy.

C. PERCUSSION

1. Each percussion instrument is listed on the left side of the line it is using. This line is reserved for that instrument until it is relabeled.

2. The timpani part appears above the other percussion parts on the score. Next are the pitched, then the unpitched percussion instruments.

3. The meter signature, clef, dynamics, metronome markings
   and key signature (for pitched instruments, except for the
   timpani) must be included.

4. There is a clef sign for unpitched instruments.

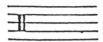

5. Certain instruments are assigned a special line on the staff.

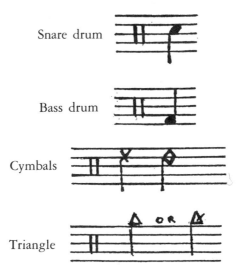

Snare drum

Bass drum

Cymbals

Triangle

6. Crowding must be avoided. Usually two instruments on a
   staff is enough. (Cymbal note-heads are sometimes added
   to the stem of the snare drum note.) The stems of notes for
   one instrument must stay pointed in the same direction to
   show that these notes belong to that instrument.

7. A line may be added for a non-pitched instrument.
   Example:

   Timpani in E, A

   Tambourine

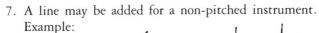
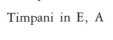

8. Different sizes of an instrument (for example, wood blocks) produce different sounds, even though they are unpitched.

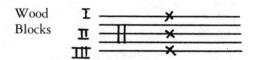

The use of staves of 2, 3 or 4 lines for unpitched percussion instruments is common.

9. Tremolo for percussion uses the same symbols as other instruments do; for example a drumroll (an unmeasured tremolo symbol for the drumroll).

Connect notes with a tie for several measures of unaccented tremolo.

10. *L.V.* (let vibrate) is often used for the cymbals if they are not to be dampened. This symbol is also used: 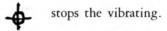 .If the note is to be very short, it is written with the word *sec* (dry):

 stops the vibrating.

11. The timpani are pitched. They use the bass clef. There is no key signature with it.

12. A short slur starting at the note may be attached to nothing, indicating a long vibrating note.

13. A part is needed for each stand because a player may have to move to another stationary instrument.

D. VOICE

1. In vocal music, notes are written before words so that the notes will have the proper spacing.

2. For the sake of the flow of the text, bars of rest should be separately indicated.

3. Each vocal part has a staff in choral music in this order:

    Soprano
    Alto
    Tenor
    Bass

    The bar lines are restricted to one staff because of the text.

4. A vocal part with an orchestra is placed above the strings in the score.

5. A note with the value of less than a quarter-note is not beamed, traditionally, on the staff for the singer; it has a flag. This may be different from the accompanying instrumental music which must show metric division.

6. Punctuation in the text must be included. Exclamation marks, etc., are written immediately after the word.

7. All directions are written above the staff, since the words are underneath.

8. Spoken words with which the pitch is not exact and which are spoken in rhythm are indicated by a cross on the stem of the note. Notes for this may utilize a single staff or line and will approximate the pitch of the spoken words.

9. Some vocal parts have a definite rhythm and pitch; some have approximate pitches but no definite rhythm; some have definite rhythm but no pitch; and some are completely free. A single line with words underneath may be used for a text that has rhythm but no pitch.
Example:

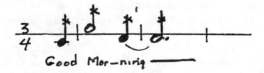

A blank staff is used when the vocal part is free; the length of time is accounted for by bar lines.

10. Hyphens are used to divide words. A long hyphen extends the word.

11. Slurs are used to show singing on one breath. An apostrophe over the staff may also show a place to take a breath.

E.   INSTRUMENTS USING MORE THAN ONE STAFF

1. Double staff instruments (piano, harp, harpsichord and celesta) use two staves joined together at the beginning of the line with a brace and a line.
Example:

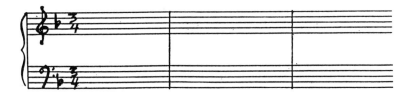

a.   The harp

• The harp has seven strings in each octave.

• At the base of the harp there are seven pedals (with letter names) which control the pitches of the strings. Each pedal has three positions: the highest position elicits the flatted note; the note is natural when the pedal is in the middle position and is sharp when the pedal is in the lowest position. The order of the pedals are D C B (on the left and operated by the left foot) and E F G A (on the right and operated by the right foot).

• The basic key is C-flat major.

• The strings are pitched so that a run of consecutive tones or arpeggios can be played with one stroke. In the case of skipped tones some strings may have to be tuned enharmonically.

- Flat keys produce the most resonance. Therefore, the flat keys are preferred. An example is G flat instead of F sharp.

- Presenting the pedal settings.
  If there is no setting shown at the beginning but there is a key signature, it is assumed that the pedals will be set according to that key. There are three ways to indicate other settings at the beginning of a composition or section (this is indicated either under or between the double staff).
  —The letters are listed and represent the pedals. These are presented in the same order as the pedals.

  ♮ ♮ ♭ ♭ ♮ ♮ ♮
  D C B E F G A

  —The most commonly used method is the diagram below. Marks above the line indicate flats; those on the line, naturals; those below the line, sharps.

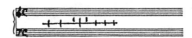

  —The letters are written in two groups, the right pedals being above, and the left below.

  E^b F G A
  B^b C D

- Changing the pedal settings.
  The change is shown by writing the letter of the note that is to be altered at the point of change or at the rest before the change. (This gives the harpist a little extra time to change the setting.) It is best to place it in the least crowded place.

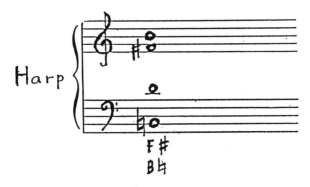

- In glissandos, usually at least two octaves long, only one octave need be written out. The glissando sign is used for extension and repetition. Sixteenths, thirty-seconds or sixty-fourths may be used.

- Harmonics are indicated by one of two methods:

  —A small circle is placed over the note which is shown at actual pitch.

  —A small circle is placed over the note which is an octave lower than the pitch to be produced. This method must be made clear at the beginning.

- A bracket is used when there is to be no roll between notes.

- A harpist can stretch to an interval of a tenth usually.

- Crescendo and decrescendo marks may follow the direction of a series of notes.

- *"Sons étouffés"* is used to signify the dampening of sound. *"L.v."* (laissez vibrer) means to "let vibrate."

b. Tempo signs are placed over the staff. Other directions, such as those for dynamics, appear between and under the two staves unless there is too much crowding.

c. Pedal marks are placed under the lower staff.

d. Bar lines go through both staves.

e. Each staff includes a clef sign and a key signature. The meter signature must appear at the beginning and at each change (except in some contemporary music which, in addition, may have no key signature because of very frequent key changes).

2. The triple staff instrument (the organ).

a. Organ music has three staves, joined with one line. The two top staves for the manuals are connected by a brace as well. The pedal staff is not included in the brace. Bar lines connect the manual staves.

b. Registration is indicated at the extreme top left above the first written tempo direction. Changes during the music are shown where needed. The registers are called

   Echo organ
   Solo organ
   Positive organ
   Choir organ
   Swell organ
   Great organ
   Pedal organ

Couplers link one manual to another or to the pedal organ.

c. The tempo is indicated above the top staff.

d. Other directions are placed between and under the staves and where needed.

e. Pedal indications for the production of bass tones are **∧** (for the toe) and **∪** (for the heel). When applying to the left foot, the direction is placed under the pedal staff. When applying to the right foot, it is over the pedal staff. This is used primarily to help the student.

PART VI: CONTEMPORARY MUSIC

A. NEW "SERIOUS" MUSIC

   1. Types of notation.

   a. Traditional method, having the metric concept of meters and beats. Traditional symbols are used.

   b. Tempered notation in which traditional symbols are changed. They are simplified as well as made more complex.

   c. Traditional metric concept with specified periods of improvisation within certain guidelines.

   d. Proportional concept, which has evolved as an extremely important idea. The notation is not exact, but proportional. Visual notation and spacing is used to show duration of time.

   e. Qualitative notation which frees the performer by using approximate notation. However, within that system, determined by the composer, that notation becomes standard for that composition.

   f. Action notation which is used when the only way to obtain the desired result is to describe the means by which the performer can produce music. Symbols may be visual or verbal.

   g. Music graphics, a method which used drawings to suggest the desired result. This allows for more freedom of interpretation than would occur with specific symbols. It may be used in combination with other types of notation.

2. The "Equitone" system is an interesting example of a system of notation. It was developed by Erhard Karkoschka, originally devised by Rodney Fawcett. It is a system in which traditional notation of pitch and duration are altered for contemporary music. It involves the concept of space and time.

   a. Pitch

      • Space between two lines represents an octave. There can be as many additional lines as needed for additional octaves. The octave is identified at the beginning by the number; e.g., C_4.

         —Only six levels of notes are between the lines. But on each level there can be black and/or white notes, half-shaded notes, differently shaped notes (triangle, square, round, etc.) to indicate microtones and semitones.

   b. Duration

      • Spacing of notes and extended lines are used to indicate duration. The extended line is usually drawn in the case of notes lasting more than one beat.

      • There are traditional beats and bar lines. Dotted bar lines are used for metric subdivisions. (Approximate values can easily be incorporated into this system by doing away with the bar lines.)

      • A rest is indicated at its beginning, and ends at the next note.

   c. The value of the Equitone system.

      • It saves space and is, therefore, economical and convenient.

      • The same tones at different octaves are easily identifiable.

      • There are no accidentals.

- The way in which pitch and duration are graphically illustrated makes this system precise and legible.

- It suggests the fact there is room for new and better systems.

3. New types of music presenting special notational problems.

    a. Electronic music.

- The sources of sound may be natural or manufactured, nonmusical or musical, nonelectronic or electronic.

- If the music is composed on tape, there is no notation. (However, to obtain a copyright, some form of written manuscript must be submitted.)

- The performance may be completely electronic or combined with live performance.

- Electronic music is microtonal since it is dependent on tone generators and tape speeds.

- There are basically two types of electronic music:

    —Musique Concrète in which nonelectronic sources of sound are recorded on tape and the work is then composed electronically.

    —Pure electronic music in which the sources are electronic as is the method of composition and performance.

    b. Minimalization, which uses a very small amount of composed and notated material, but which becomes a full composition by suggesting to the listener a situation about which to think, instructing the performers to repeat the motifs or to progress from one kind of instrument to another playing the same piece of music, demanding silence in order to hear physical or imaginary sounds, etc.

    c. Chance music in which the performance of the music is unpredictable. The composer may use graphic, traditional, tempered and verbal instructions.

4. Some requirements for new music notation.

   a. Illustrations, verbal instructions and symbols should be used in combination as little as possible. (Symbols should not need verbal explanations.)

   b. Symbols should be easily recognizable. (*New Music Vocabulary* by Howard Risatti is a very extensive and comprehensive book on the subject of symbols for new music. It includes general material as well as that specifically for each group of instruments.)

   c. There should be only one meaning per symbol.

   d. A new system of notation should be employed only

      • if the traditional system is inadequate.

      • for the problems of contemporary music (for example, approximate values, clusters, microtones and limiting of freedom through the use of meters and bar lines).

5. Changes in notation for contemporary music. The following books are excellent for information on new notation:

   New Music Notation by David Cope
   New Music Composition by David Cope
   New Music Vocabulary by Howard Risatti
   Music Notation by Gardner Read (each chapter has a section at the end called, "Modern Innovations")

   a. Note-heads.

      • The shape of the note may signify the duration. Example:  hold the note until the sound fades to the amount needed.

      • The size of the note may indicate the degree of loudness.

b. Stems.

Stems are used with or without note-heads, flags and beams. Without note-heads but with flags and/or beams the stems indicate pulsation. Unisons with accidentals (which are to be played simultaneously) present a special problem which may be solved in this way: accidentals are placed before each note, both stems go up or down towards each other and then form one stem forming a Y. Example:

An adjacent note may be added. Example:

If two voices are involved, stems going in opposite directions would be clearer. In this case a bracket is placed over or under the notes. Example:

The practice of one stem for two notes with both accidentals before the notes is less clear but may be used. Example:

In the case of a group of more than two notes played together and which includes an altered unison, notes are joined with a single stem, except for the second not usually on the stem. Because of the need for space for the accidental, the stem is slanted in order to be joined to the vertical stem. Example:

c. Flags.
Short individual beams may be substituted for flags. Example:

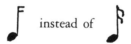 instead of

d. Rests.
In a score, rests are not used in a measure when a part is silent for a page. Instead, the measures are left blank. Some composers do use whole rests for those parts that are silent but that play in other measures of that page.

e. Clefs.

Clefs are sometimes written in unusual ways:

• Unusual placement.

• Placement once on top staff and line drawn through other staves to show they use the same clef.

• In many cases no clef symbols appear for instruments that use only one clef.

• There are simplified versions of the alto/tenor and bass clefs symbols.
Example:

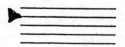

f. Staff.

• Usually the traditional arrangement is used, although there have been novel ideas suggested. These have never become popular, however.

• Because there is so much new music with extreme distances between notes which are played by an instrument, ledger lines and octave signs appear frequently.

g. Brackets and frames (rectangular boxes).

• Brackets and braces which join staves are employed in the traditional way.

• Brackets and braces are sometimes used to enclose notes which are to be played as fast as possible.

• One way with which to notate altered unisons is to use a bracket. (See page 86.)

• Frames and improvisation.
Improvisational material is enclosed in frames. In proportional notation the length of the horizontal side of the frame plus the duration line is the indication of the duration of the improvisation period. A note or number (representing seconds) above this may be inserted to give a more exact idea of the duration.

Composers may require improvisation in some areas while, at the same time, give strict instructions about others. The areas include dynamics, articulation, rhythm, and pitches, for example. When no pitches are specified, only stems are written, usually when the notes are to be played as fast as possible (AFAP). Heavy frame lines usually indicate that there will be a thick musical texture. Examples:

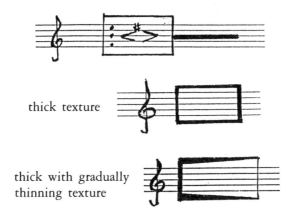

thick texture

thick with gradually thinning texture

Some symbols:

pitch to be approximated

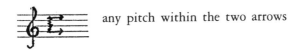 any pitch within the two arrows

freedom to choose the dynamics

h. Key signatures.
In avant garde music it is quite customary for a composition to have a diminished feeling of tonality or to be atonal. Changes from one tonal center to another are often not at all subtle or gradual. Therefore, many works have no key signatures. Other compositions have many changes in key signatures and, for this reason, it is no longer necessary to cancel out the old

key before writing in the new one, except in a change to the key of C. Another new practice is to have mixed signatures of sharps and flats either on the same staff, or on different staves, but at the same point in the music.

i.   Time signatures.

   • Large meter marks often cover several staves for the sake of convenience and easy reading.

   • A note is sometimes substituted for the bottom number of the meter marking.

   • Some composers use only the top number, the bottom number is understood.

   • Meter symbols may have additional information. An illustration of this would be $\frac{3^+}{4}$ which means that there is an additional fraction of a beat.

j.   Rhythm.
   Rhythm may be just as strict as in traditional music,

but there is much notation for varying degrees of freedom not given in traditional music. A combination of the metric and proportional systems works very well. Some new practices are as follows:

• Bar lines.

—Bar lines are drawn in proportional notation to give reference points in time so that the performers will play together. The idea is to do away with dependence on the tyranny of the meter, beats and accents. The bar lines are spaced a specific distance apart (often the distance represents the number of seconds in which the notes are played). This method helps the composer to simplify the notation and allows for more flexibility.

—Dotted bar lines may be drawn to make clear subdivisions of rhythm and groupings of notes. (Dotted bar lines may be drawn for directions in voice leading, progression of instruments, etc. and not only for division of a measure. See below.)

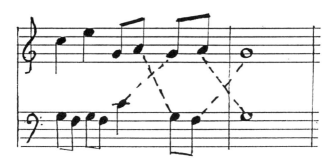

—They are also drawn in to mark the point of a sudden change in tempo.

• Duration.

—Space between notes is the key to the duration of the note. The group of notes must be played within a definite amount of time, as specified in the beginning of the work.

—The shape of the note may signify the duration of the note. See page 85.

—Extended beams may show duration. Example:

—Numbers are often written above the note or passage to indicate duration. This represents the number of seconds involved.

—In proportional notation, a thick line, the width of a space is drawn from a note. The length of the line indicates the duration of the note, chord, a group of repeated notes or a frame for an improvisational purpose. The period of time is proportional to the time of the composition or section of the work. (See page 88.)

—Slurs are sometimes used to indicate duration. The note sounds until the end of the slur.

k. Beams.

• The most important new practice of notation is beaming over the bar lines. This is much more practical than the traditional way because of the prevalence of syncopation and unusual rhythmic arrangements. When this occurs at the end of a line, the beam extends past the last note of that line, and starts before the first note of the next line.

• Beams include rests even if the rests are at the beginning or end of the group. Example:

- Short beams instead of flags are used. The beams are easier to draw.

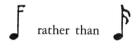 rather than

- Many contemporary composers employ beaming to show accelerando and ritardando in the following way:

ritardando

accelerando

- Beaming is used for an approximation of the duration of the note, but spacing rather than beams or flags indicates duration. ⌐‾ʼ The arrow shows how long the sound should last.

1. Tempo.

  - Tempo markings may be specific or may give the performer the choice within certain limits. The following example is fairly specific:

  ♩ = 60-64

  - Metronomic markings rather than verbal directions should always appear at the beginning of a work. The following marking gives freedom to choose a tempo between limits of 65 and 80, hovering around 72:

In addition, verbal directions describing the mood desired may be written near those metronomic markings.

- Sudden changes of tempo should occur near the bar line. If that is not possible, a dotted bar line should mark the point of change.

- Most often a measured distance in space represents the time value. $\underset{\longleftrightarrow}{4''}$ means that the notes which extend for that distance are to be played in four seconds.

- A few symbols and terms
  —As fast as possible   AFAP

Senza tempo means change to free tempo. This term is often written when changing from strict metric to proportional notation.

Accelerando and ritardando.
(See page 93.)
Others:

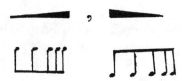

m. Pitch.

- Pitch symbols may represent approximate pitches and pitches relative to each other.

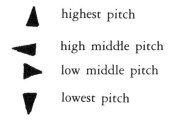

highest pitch

high middle pitch

low middle pitch

lowest pitch

- A stem without a note-head means that there is no definite pitch.

However, the line of the stems is to be followed. An "X" instead of a note-head means that the pitch is approximate.

This method allows the rhythm to be shown.

- An example of an octave sign is $\mathbf{15\uparrow}$ (two octaves higher).

- The melodic line may be diagrammed to show pitches, the notes to be played in any direction.

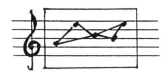

- Microtones
  There are many more symbols for accidentals in new
  music than in traditional music since tones are often
  altered by intervals of one-quarter or less. These are
  called "microtones." There are many different systems of notation for microtones.
  Example:

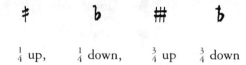

$\frac{1}{4}$ up, $\frac{1}{4}$ down, $\frac{3}{4}$ up $\frac{3}{4}$ down

In some cases, an instrument may be tuned to a
microtone scale. In fact there is an attempt to invent
instruments with the express purpose of accom-
modating the microtone scale.

David Cope's idea, as expressed in *New Music Notation*, page 28, that to be exact, microtones might be
notated with the cents system. Since there are 100
cents between each semitone (a semitone would be
1.00), the three-quarter tone would be .75. The
numbers would be written above the note if it is to
be raised; below, if it is to be lowered.

An example:

- Clusters
  A "cluster" is a chromatic progression of notes
  played simultaneously. There are many ways to notate a cluster. One that is used frequently is a double
  stem or heavy vertical line drawn between the lowest
  and the highest notes. An accidental may be placed
  above to indicate the use of only sharps, flats or

naturals; "black keys" or "white keys" may be written instead.

Some times a bracket is drawn. The bottom end of the bracket may be substituted for the middle C ledger line.

- There are special symbols for unusual clusters. Examples:

 The lower notes start first.

 a cluster glissando with all flatted notes. (The pitches are written below.)

It is helpful to write out the desired notes of the cluster on the score.

n. Dynamics are indicated in the traditional way, if possible. If more subtle degrees are desired, the composer may add more "p's" and "f's" (ppppp, ff, etc.). These symbols may also be written in new ways: for example,

mf/f which means that there is a choice of either

mf or *f* . Verbal directions are very often needed as well.

Because there is more gradation of dynamics, there is need for more symbols. Many composers devise their own systems, since there is as yet no standard system. One practical method is to have the size of the note-head indicate the degree of loudness, particularly in a progression of notes. Numbers are often preferred to the old system. If this or any other new system is used, there must be an explanation before the first page of the composition.

Example of utilizing the size of note-heads:

o. Layouts should conform as much as possible to those used traditionally without undermining the ideas of the composer. Any new format or deviation from a traditional format should include a guide to the performer at the beginning of the composition. (See EXCERPTS OF MUSIC MANUSCRIPTS AND COMPOSERS' COMMENTS, pages 123–187.)

p. Repetitions.

   • Some symbols of repetitions:

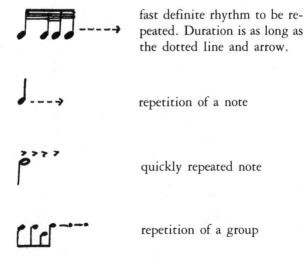

fast definite rhythm to be repeated. Duration is as long as the dotted line and arrow.

repetition of a note

quickly repeated note

repetition of a group

two-finger tremolo extends to
the end of the horizontal line.

q. Arpeggios and chords.
Some examples of notation:

- Chord. A bracket is used to show that the chord is
  not broken, especially if, because of the spread between the lowest and the highest notes, the player
  might be tempted to play it as an arpeggio.

- 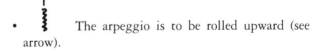 The arpeggio is rolled in either direction.

- The arpeggio is to be rolled upward (see
  arrow).

r. The new notation for instruments is much more graphic than that for traditional music. Verbal directions
   abound because of many practices, such as inserting
   objects between the strings, using the harmonics of a
   string, tone clusters (see page 96), playing on the
   strings, lids, sounding boards, etc. The symbols are
   also many, varied and very helpful. Some are more
   commonly used than others, but there is still no standard notation for the majority of new practices.
   Example:

   Piano

   Place book on specific strings

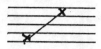

Harp

Play with the fingernails near the sounding board.

Organ

Turn off the organ with the keys depressed. A glissando will be produced.

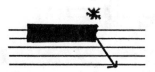

Strings

Bow direction changed

Percussion

Tambourine

Maracas

Whip

Circular motion, gradually getting faster

Woodwinds

Hold the tone until a breath is expired.

Brass

Open gradually.

Voice

Cup hand in front of mouth.

Amplified sound

Reverb on

Reverb off

Conductor

A beat which may be omitted.

For a very extensive guide to notational signs for contemporary music, see *New Music Vocabulary* by Howard Risatti.

B. EXCERPTS OF MUSIC MANUSCRIPTS AND COMPOS-
   ERS' COMMENTS.

A composer may use his or her own system for contemporary music, but it is advantageous to the performer, and, therefore, to the composer, to further the establishment of a universal notation system for this kind of music. There are many systems already in use. In most systems the usual procedure for directions that are specifically for one particular piece of music and which apply to that music generally is to discuss those directions on the page preceding the first page of music. Some composers give directions as the work proceeds. There is often a page diagramming the special placement of instruments for the performance.

This author has concluded that the combination of traditional and new notation is the most practical way to proceed. Since traditional symbols are so well known and serviceable, they should be used when at all possible.

The Appendix (pages 000–000) includes sample manuscripts that illustrate the range of preferences composers have in contemporary notation. Often, a composer will base his choice on the type of work. It is interesting and helpful to read some statements by composers on this subject, as well as their directions before and during the work.

C. "POPULAR MUSIC" (jazz, folk, country, blues, etc.)
   "Popular music" follows the same general rules for notation and preparation of manuscripts as does traditional music. However, there are certain practices that are peculiar to popular music which the composer and copyist should know.

   1. Clef signs are often left out after the first line when dealing with instrumental parts, since each instrument uses only one clef.

2. Key signatures are included.

3. Time signatures are usually simple. Jazz, particularly, emphasizes improvisation and syncopation. The basic time and notes are written down. Slashes are used for instruments such as guitar, ukelele, vibraphones ("vibes"), drums, string bass and piano. The time signatures used ordinarily are $\frac{4}{4}$ and $\frac{2}{4}$.

4. A method of using a *multiple rest sign* is different from the traditional one. A heavy line with cap lines at the ends is drawn on the middle line of the first measure of the group of measures in which the instrument rests. The measures after the first are left blank.

A slanted multiple rest sign is drawn to indicate an improvised solo. The lower end cap of the line is drawn between the first and the third lines, the top cap between the third and the fifth lines. The number of bars of the "break" is written over the stave.

5. There are not many subtle distinctions in dynamics. Often the dynamics depend on the group's or soloist's inclination.

6. To indicate a "break" for improvising, the following method is used:

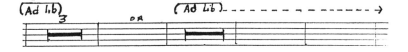

Improvisation is the act of creating freely within a certain time frame. Other directions may be added; for example, harmonic progressions, dynamics, etc. ("Ad lib" or "fill" are two of the terms which indicate that improvisation is required.)

7. Often "col" and the name of the instrument followed by a wavy line indicates the doubling of a part.

8. When a special effect is desired, the term is written or the symbol is drawn.
   Examples: "growl"

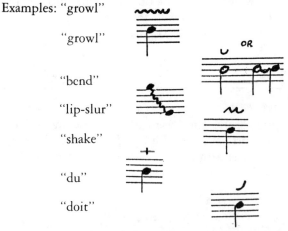

   "growl"

   "bend"

   "lip-slur"

   "shake"

   "du"

   "doit"

9. Transposing may be required in certain circumstances; for example, for less professional vocalists not able to sing in the original key.

10. Substitution of instruments with other instruments is sometimes necessary; for example, a night club orchestra may not include the instruments called for in the original score. A clarinet may substitute for an alto flute; a bass clarinet for a viola, a cello or bassoon; a trombone for a French horn.

11. Lead sheets.
    Lead sheets are simplified copies of songs prepared for the

composer to give the performers, Copyright Office, recording companies, etc.. They are usually hand-written and have one-staved lines with melody notes and chord symbols. (Sometimes chord diagrams are included.) Transparencies are used. It is important to keep the master copy for future use.

Lead sheets must include the following points:

a. At the top.

  • Title (centered above the music)

  • Name of the composer (above the last bar of the first line)

  • Name of the lyricist (above the first bar of the first line of music, and above the tempo or style direction)

b. The name, address and telephone number of the composer should appear somewhere on the bottom of the same page.

c. A copyright notice must appear on the bottom of the first page.
  Example: © 1987 Mona Mender
    or © 1987 Publishing Company

d. The treble clef is used.

e. Both the the key signature and the meter signature must be included.

f. First and second endings and Dal Segno short cuts may be utilized.

g. Notes and measures should be as evenly spaced as possible. Crowding, of course, is to be avoided. Ample room should be left for the lyrics, which are written directly under the appropriate notes.

h. To show that the word or syllable must be held, draw a horizontal line from the syllable or word to the end of the holding period.

i.   The chord symbols must be exactly above the first of
     the group of notes to which it applies.

Example:

(COPYRIGHT INFORMATION)

(Composer's name, address and telephone number)

12. Song copies.
    Song copies follow the same rules as lead sheets. (See page
    104.) In addition, a set of double staves is added below the
    vocal line so that the accompaniment may be written.

20

Recorded by HERB ALPERT & THE TIJUANA BRASS

A TASTE OF HONEY

Words by
RIC MARLOW

Music l
BOBBY SC

Copyright © 1960 & 1962 SONGFEST MUSIC,CORP., 1650 Broadway, New York. N.Y. 10019
Sole Selling Agent: GEORGE PINCUS & SONS MUSIC CORP.
International Copyright Secured   Made in U.S.A.   All Rights Reserved

By permission

13. Band scores (including music for jazz and rock groups).

    a. Each type of instrument has a separate part. The soloist has a separate part. Each part has the name of the instrument in the upper right corner, the title in the top center, the tempo or style above the first measure of the first line, the composer and arranger above the last measure of the first line and the copyright information on the bottom of the page.

    b. There is a full score for the conductor.
       Example:

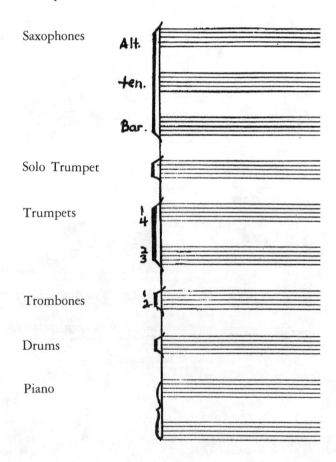

    c. "Vibes" (vibraphone), piano, drums and string bass often form a group within the larger jazz ensemble; therefore, a bracket is drawn to group their staves together. (This group is placed between the winds and the strings in a large group.)

14. Parts

    a. The conductor part.
       The conductor part is a condensed version of the score. This saves frequent page-turning. It is used for arrangements for night clubs, concerts, etc. In the recording session, the conductor usually prefers the full score first. The producer and, often, the engineer want the conductor parts. (The part then is called "production part" or "booth" part.) In the case of motion pictures and film television recordings the music editor requires the conductor part to check on timing and to put the music track on the film. In the case of the conductor part, which requires a double staff, these practices are followed:

- All pertinent information must be included.

- A three-sided box often encloses the name of the instrument which has an entrance. Example:

$$\overline{(\mathcal{S} \times \mathcal{S}}$$

- An attempt is made to make the measures fairly evenly matched in length.
- Lyrics are placed above the notes.
- A boxed tempo direction appears above the vocal line.
- Bar numbers are boxed and placed between the two staves and in the middle of the measure.
- Note-heads are smaller and stems shorter than those usually used.
- The notes in the orchestral line are often irregularly

spaced because of the problem of matching syllables to notes.

- The instruments are distributed on the two staves; therefore, each individual line is made clearer by having all the stems of that line point in the same direction, as in "divisi."

- If the arrangement is very simple, it may be written on one staff.
  More than two staves may be necessary for a line if there are many instruments performing.

- The orchestral line is notated in the treble clef for a double-staved system. If it is to sound lower, "8va bassa" may be written to indicate this.
  Example: A layout of a conductor part for concert band music.

(Copyright information)

b. Piano-conductor part.
Night club acts require the piano-conductor part. Just as in the case of a song copy, three staves are needed. The vocal line is on the upper staff. The lyrics are written above the notes. The chord symbols are placed between the piano staves. As many cues as possible are included. Rests and slashes (instead of chords) may be used on the piano part to help avoid clutter.

c. Chorus parts.
One part is printed for every two singers. The lyrics are written between the staves; therefore, they are written only twice for three staves.

Three voices may be on one line. It must be stated at the beginning exactly how many singers will sing each part. When there is a change, it must be so indicated. Dynamics must be shown on each line.
Singers prefer beamed notes rather than flags.

d. The percussion part.
In the cueing of instruments in the percussion part, one single line may be drawn above the staff to give the rhythm of the other instruments. Wire brushes on the drums or cymbals are often used. The symbol is ✗ .

When sticks are used, the symbol is a diamond-shaped note-head. ◇

Most percussion parts have repetitions of a measure. Repeat signs make this clear and emphasize a change when it occurs. It is advisable to have eight measures to a line, whenever possible.

e. The piano part.

- The piano part may be written out as in classical or traditional music, but often the chord symbols appear between the two staves; the top staff has slash marks for the right hand (sometimes there is a chord and then slash marks for repetitions of that chord); the staff for the left hand may have only bass notes.

- Single or double measure repetition signs are used only if they occur in both hands; otherwise it is too difficult to read. When used, they are written on both staves.

- When cueing a vocal part into the piano part, the vocal line is often written higher than it sounds. This part is on the same staff as the right hand piano chords.

- In music for night clubs, it is important to cue in important information, such as interludes, modulations and endings.

- When no melody is required on the piano or electric piano, specific notes are not shown. Instead chord symbols and slashes are used to indicate the rhythm. Only one staff is needed for a line. This may change to the usual double staff on the next line; but not in the middle of a line.

• Extended arpeggios may be written in this way:

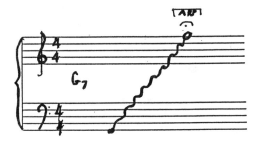

f. Violin and piano part.

• Paper should be used which has staves far enough apart from each other to allow for ledger lines.

• The violin line has cue notes, instead of the normal-sized notes.

• In popular music, often all violin parts are written on one part and are designated A, B, C and D violins. One set of stems for two violin parts is usual, except in cases of unisons, seconds, large intervals and difficult pairing because of rhythm and obvious counterpoint.

g. Vocal part.

• Words must be properly hyphenated.

• Single and double-repetition signs are not used in vocal parts; nor are first and second endings and Dal Segno. These must be written out completely. (They may be used, however, in lead sheets.)

• A ruler should be employed when printing words. The words and syllables must be directly below the accompanying notes. Hyphens separate words and syllables. Extended hyphens are also drawn, usually to signify the extended sound of the voice.

15. Guitar music for folk, jazz and other "popular" music.

a. Chord diagram notation is used to represent the chord
    to be played. Unless otherwise stated, the top horizon-
    tal line represents the nut; the other horizontal lines
    represent the frets starting with the first fret near the
    nut. The six vertical lines symbolize the strings. (Note
    that the lines for the strings extend past the last fret in
    the diagram to show that there are more frets.)

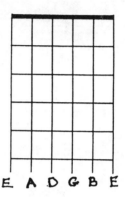

b. Numbers for fingering, when included, are usually
    written over each string to be played. *1* is the index
    finger; *2*, the middle finger; *3*, the ring finger; and *4*,
    the little finger.

c. A small circle indicates an open string.

d. If no fingering or no circle appears over the string, that
    string is not to be used.

e. The small black dot shows where the string is to be
    pressed.

f. A slur is used to show that one fingertip presses on
    more than one string at the same fret. This is called
    "barré." A "grand barré" means that the first finger
    presses on all strings.

g. The name of each chord (chord symbol) is written over
    the diagram.

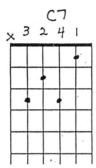

h. A chord symbol must not cross a bar line.

i. A black diamond in the diagram, fingered, represents a bass note, but a white diamond over the strings in the place usually reserved for fingering indicates that the string is open for that bass note.

j. ⊗ above a string means that a string is to be touched to mute it.

k. Notation on the staff.

- A slash between the second and fourth lines is used when a chord is to be repeated on the beat and when the guitar has no melody line. (A slash is equal to a quarter-note.)

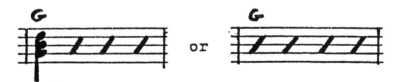

or

- Stems must be drawn on the slash when the notes are not quarter-notes.

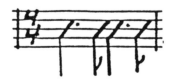

- Diamond note-heads instead of slashes are used for half-notes, dotted half-notes and whole notes.

- Music is notated one octave higher than it sounds.

l. Indications for accents, etc. are placed under the staff because of chord symbols and diagrams above the staff.

- ➤ indicates that the strings are strummed with a slight accent.

- ◡ means to strum lightly.

- ⊓ is the symbol for the use of the down stroke.

m. Lyrics are written underneath a single staff unless there are staves for other guitars, piano, etc.

n. The order of instruments for jazz guitar is from high to low in range.

o. Tablature is a very important new method of notation using a six-line staff. The lines represent the strings of a guitar. The numbers on the strings represent the frets. Directly above is the traditional five-line staff with the corresponding traditional notation. This method is particularly helpful for the guitarist who does not have training in reading classical notation.

16. Banjo.
    The banjo has five strings. In the tablature system of notation, the six-line staff is used. The numbers of the frets are placed in the *spaces* between the lines. Fingering is written below the staff.

17. Ukulele, dulcimer, fiddle, mandolin and bass guitar. These instruments use the four inner lines of the six-lined staff.

PART VII: PROOFREADING
BY WAY OF COUNTING MEASURES

The score is outlined in the following way:

A. At each important point the number of bars up to that point are marked down, but not more than ten bars at a time may be unmarked.

B. The important points are as follows:

1. Tempo changes.

2. Meter signature changes.

3. Rehearsal numbers.

4. Number of bars of rests.

5. Number of bars of repetition.

C. The score must be checked.

D. Each part must be checked against the measure count of the score.

E. The measure number is placed above the staff left of center in the measure. The number is enclosed in a parenthesis. Rehearsal numbers are in boxes. The number of bars of rest or of each bar of repetition is placed over the staff, in the middle of the bar, or (as in the case of a double staff in music for a piano, for example) between the two staves without an enclosure.

F. A chart should be made when counting measures to check each part against the score. An example is as follows:

Instrumental part	Part checked	Name of checker
1. Flute	✔	John Smith
2. Oboe	✔	Jane Doe
3.		

G. It is very helpful in checking parts to have a page with bar numbers, tempo changes, etc. against which to check the parts instead of having to go through the score.

H. A mistake is corrected in the margin and a line drawn to the mistake.

PART VIII: DUPLICATION OF MANUSCRIPTS

A. The black-and-white process (DIAZO PROCESS) which is used by commercial printing firms.

   1. This is used for a relatively small number of copies.

   2. Transparencies (translucent manuscript paper) are used. The notation is done on the blank side, not on the side with the staves. This is done so that one does not erase the lines when erasing other things. This is the master copy used in the duplicating process.

   3. This is the process usually preferred by composers.

B. An OFFSET PRINTING MACHINE produces a large number of copies.

C. OFFICE COPYING MACHINES may be used, but the machine must be large enough to accommodate the music manuscript page for the master copy.

D. BINDING

   1. Music reproduction companies generally offer a binding service.

   2. If the composer wishes to bind the pages, this can be done.

     a. It is advisable to use both sides of a page (not in the master copy) to keep the score less bulky.

b. Stapling or sewing may be the method if there are not too many pages. Music is written on both sides of the page. This method is used mostly by singers since they have both hands free to hold the music in place.

c. Separate pages may be attached and folded in an accordian manner. These must have the music written on only one side so that all the pages lie side by side and no pages have to be turned.

d. Strong tape, preferably cloth may be obtained for this purpose.

e. A simple loose-leaf book may be enough in some cases.

E. To obtain information about the COPYRIGHT LAW write to
Copyright Office
The Library of Congress
Washington, D.C. 20559

APPENDIX:
SAMPLE MUSIC MANUSCRIPTS

1. ALLEN BONDE

I am quite aware of new and novel concepts of 20th-century music notation and its symbolic usage, and I occasionally draw from these ideas and implications in order to expand more fully my compositional procedures. If, however, the traditional means of Western notation suffice in order to regulate my creativity, I almost invariably use those gestures with comfort and assurance that standard symbols will serve as the necessary "guidelines" for a faithful yet spontaneous performance of my music. More importantly, for me, is the specific articulation called for in my scores. Students frequently pay little attention to, or simply ignore the importance of precise indications of dynamics, accent and stress marks, phrasing, etc. in developing their musical projections. Performers must enjoy a certain license in their interpretive spirit; but I find that they generally prefer a complete and exacting measure of the composer's intent, rather than a casual and uncertain display. *Fanfare for Elizabeth* demonstrates my compulsion for clarity in this regard. This is especially true in the ensemble pages. Professionals tend to be more concerned and involved with articulation even as part and parcel of the overall structure of a piece of music. I always remind my composition students, from the absolute beginner to the advanced, that they must think of themselves as "professionals" in every aspect.

ALLEN BONDE
Professor of Music
Mount Holyoke College
South Hadley, MA

For Elizabeth Topham Kennan, President, Mount Holyoke College.

ALLEN BONDE

FANFARE FOR ELIZABETH

Six Trumpets in C or B♭, with optional Timpani

SCHAFFNER PUBLISHING COMPANY

Merchantville, NJ 08109-0162

Used by permission.

For Elizabeth T. Kennan, President, Mount Holyoke College.

FANFARE FOR ELIZABETH

SCORE   ALLEN BONDE

✳ indicates point at which solo part may be divided among players for antiphonal effect.

© Copyright 1981 **SCHAFFNER PUBLISHING COMPANY**. *All Rights Reserved. Used by permission.*

SCORE

For Elizabeth Topham Kennan, President, Mount Holyoke College.

FANFARE FOR ELIZABETH

TRUMPET I   ALLEN BONDE

© Copyright 1981 **SCHAFFNER PUBLISHING COMPANY**. *All Rights Reserved.* Used by permission.

For Elizabeth T. Kennan, President, Mount Holyoke College.

FANFARE FOR ELIZABETH

TRUMPET II

ALLEN BONDE

＊indicates point at which solo part may be divided among players for antiphonal effect.

© Copyright 1981 **SCHAFFNER PUBLISHING COMPANY**. *All Rights Reserved.* Used by permission.

For Elizabeth T. Kennan, President, Mount Holyoke College.

FANFARE FOR ELIZABETH

TRUMPET III

ALLEN BONDE

✳ indicates point at which solo part may be divided among players for antiphonal effect.

© Copyright 1981 **SCHAFFNER PUBLISHING COMPANY**. *All Rights Reserved.* Used by permission.

For Elizabeth T. Kennan, President, Mount Holyoke College.

FANFARE FOR ELIZABETH

TRUMPET IV

ALLEN BONDE

✳ indicates point at which solo part may be divided among players for antiphonal effect.

© Copyright 1981 **SCHAFFNER PUBLISHING COMPANY**. *All Rights Reserved*. Used by permission.

For Elizabeth T. Kennan, President, Mount Holyoke College.

FANFARE FOR ELIZABETH

TRUMPET V   ALLEN BONDE

✻ indicates point at which solo part may be divided among players for antiphonal effect.

© Copyright 1981 **SCHAFFNER PUBLISHING COMPANY.** *All Rights Reserved.* Used by permission.

For Elizabeth T. Kennan, President, Mount Holyoke College.

FANFARE FOR ELIZABETH

TRUMPET VI   ALLEN BONDE

❋indicates point at which solo part may be divided among players for antiphonal effect.

© Copyright 1981 **SCHAFFNER PUBLISHING COMPANY**. *All Rights Reserved*. Used by permission.

For Elizabeth T. Kennan, President, Mount Holyoke College.

FANFARE FOR ELIZABETH

TIMPANI   ALLEN BONDE

USE THIS PART WHEN C TRUMPETS ARE EMPLOYED. FOR B♭ TRUMPETS SEE OTHER SIDE.

© Copyright 1981 **SCHAFFNER PUBLISHING COMPANY**. *All Rights Reserved.* Used by permission.

For Elizabeth T. Kennan, President, Mount Holyoke College.

FANFARE FOR ELIZABETH

TIMPANI   ALLEN BONDE

USE THIS PART WHEN B♭ TRUMPETS ARE EMPLOYED. FOR C TRUMPETS, SEE OTHER SIDE.

© Copyright 1981 **SCHAFFNER PUBLISHING COMPANY**. *All Rights Reserved*. Used by permission.

2. MILTON BABBITT

Herewith a few pages of my music.

It should be noted, the scores are "C scores," that is, all instruments sound as notated. Also, accidentals affect only those notes which they immediately precede, without exception.

MILTON BABBITT
Princeton University
Princeton, NJ

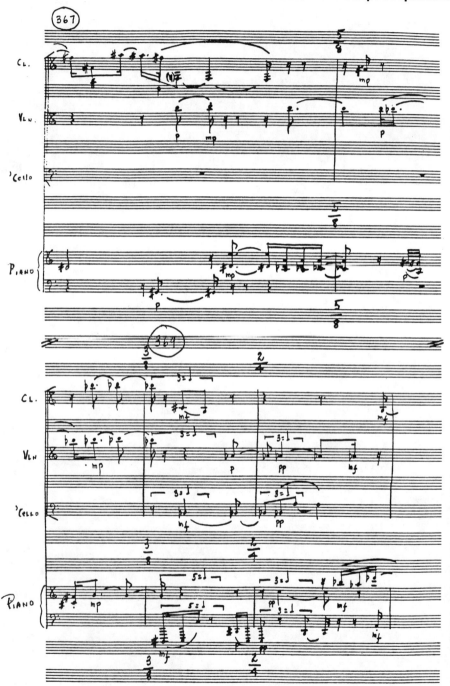

"FOUR PLAY" (1984) by Milton Babbitt. Used by permission.

3. ROBERT SUDERBURG

The main challenge in contemporary notation is to present CLEAR musical ideas, CLEARLY. I.e., to provide performer with supportive and stimulating notational cues which lead to the apt sounding-gesture, much as the script provides the performance based for the actor. Essential in this is to use traditional notation as much as is feasible, given the musical idea to be projected; and when using new symbolism, to explain its use in simple English, at the point of its use in the score/part (much as the percussionist prefers directions to be given in the part).

ROBERT SUDERBURG
Professor of Music
Williams College
Williamstown, MA

Piano Score

Concerto

for Solo Percussionist and Orchestra

Robert Suderburg

1. lament
2. lyrics
3. dance

Commissioned by and dedicated to Michael Bookspan who premiered the work on April 19, 1979 with the Philadelphia Orchestra, Eugene Ormandy conducting.

Note: Cadenzas in first and third movements (resp.: 1. — m. 218; 3. — m. 193) are suggested only. The soloist is invited to expand and/or write his own cadenzas for these places in the gestural character and timbre, as well as length, appropriate to the given movement.

Edited by Michael Bookspan

© 1984 by
THEODORE PRESSER COMPANY
Bryn Mawr, Pennsylvania 19010

Used by permission of the publisher.

Solo Percussionist

Instruments

Metal choir: 5 Suspended Cymbals [2 sm., 2 med., 1 lg.:

5 Tai Gongs:

> If Tai Gongs of different pitch levels have to be substituted, their pitches should be in close concord to those pitches indicated.

2 Tam Tams: med. / lg.

Crotales

Glockenspiel, Vibraphone

Head choir: 5 Tom Toms [sm. to lg.:

> Tom Toms tuned to a-minor triad.

Bass Drum   [B.D.

Tambourine (mounted)

Wood: Xylophone

Note: recommended stix/beater indicated in percussion part and piano score.

Setup

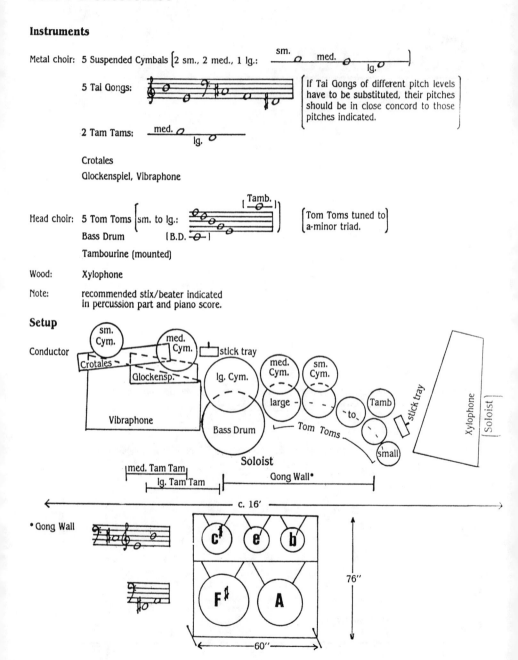

Concerto
for Solo Percussionist and Orchestra

1. lament

© 1984 by Theodore Presser Co., Bryn Mawr, Pa.
114-40388

All Rights Reserved
Printed in U.S.A.

International Copyright Secured

Unauthorized copying, arranging, adapting or recording is an infringement

Used by permission of the publisher.

Concerto
for Solo Percussionist and Orchestra

1. lament

ROBERT SUDERBURG
(1978)

© 1984 by Theodore Presser Co., Bryn Mawr, Pa.   All Rights Reserved   International Copyright Secured
114-40388   Printed in U.S.A.

> Unauthorized copying, arranging, adapting or recording is an infringement
> of copyright. Infringers are liable under the law.

Used by permission of the publisher.

Concerto

for Solo Harp and Orchestra

Robert Suderburg

I. cadenza • dark pageant • lyric
II. cadenza • night presto • meditation

Commissioned by and dedicated to Marilyn Costello, for performance with the Philadelphia Orchestra. Preview performance at
the national conference of the American Harp Society at the
North Carolina School of the Arts in Winston-Salem, June 15,
1982.

© 1982 by
THEODORE PRESSER COMPANY
Bryn Mawr, Pennsylvania 19010

Used by permission of the publisher.

CONCERTO for Solo Harp and Orchestra   by Robert Suderburg
                              INSTRUMENTATION
                    (Parts available on rental from the publisher)

          Solo Harp   Contra Bassoon
          Piccolo   4 Horns in F
        3 Flutes   3 Bb Trumpets
        2 Oboes   3 Trombones
          English Horn   Tuba
        2 Bb Clarinets   Percussion
          Bb Bass Clarinet   Timpani
        2 Bassoons   Strings

CONCERTO For Solo Harp and Orchestra   by Robert Suderburg

II CADENZA ·

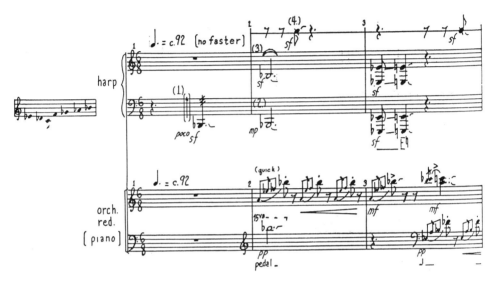

1. With fingernail, scrape-up wire-string with single rapid-motion from sound-board.

2. Pluck same string with fingertip immediately after nail-stroke.

3. "sons plectriques", fingernail very close to soundboard.

4. strike sound-board with:
   single finger [♩]; 2,3,4 fingers [♩]; knuckle [♩].

   near strings in center of sound-board, in three approximate pitch-areas : low ♩ medium ♩ high ♩.

   these pitch-areas related to approximate centers of lowest three octaves :

©1982 Theodore Presser Company. Used by permission of the publisher.

CONCERTO For Solo Harp and Orchestra   by Robert Suderburg
(two/three to measure)

©1982 Theodore Presser Company. Used by permission of the publisher.

Chamber Music III

Night Set for Trombone and Piano

Robert Suderburg

I. cry, man
II. its been a long, long time
III. brother Devil

$10.00

Theodore Presser Company
Bryn Mawr, Pennsylvania 19010

©1980 Theodore Presser Company. Used by permission of the publisher.

Composer's Note

"Being the son of a jazz and club trombonist, one recalls a
childhood filled with the coming and going of all types of
musicians at all varieties of hour. Most of all, however, it
guaranteed that the instrument itself and the way R. A. Suderburg
played it would produce sound and sight images never to be
forgotten. Thus, when commissioned by Stuart Dempster for a
Night Set for trombone, the musical occasion was offered to
let out those hot-licks and sliding-styles which were the jazz
trombonist's stock and trade during the thirties and forties
as he wandered from indoor dance hall to outdoor bandstand and
from club date to stage show. Hopefully, nurtured by Dempster's
unique performance-art, these styles and scenes can live again
in NIGHT SET, fusing memory with filial bit-of-the-devil and
sweetness with satire. Thus the work is dedicated to my father,
who — along with Stuart Dempster — should take a bow, at least
for those portions of the work which may please or amuse."

Trombone

II. its been a long, long time

©1980 Theodore Presser Company. Used by permission of the publisher.

II. its been a long, long time

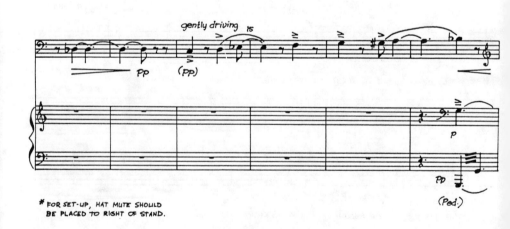

©1980 Theodore Presser Company. Used by permission of the publisher.

Dedicated to the memory of Diana Briner

Chamber Music VI
Three Movements for Viola and Double Bass

Duration: c. 15' 30"

ROBERT SUDERBURG
edited by Sally Peck and Lynn Peters

1. Dark Procession

© 1983 by Theodore Presser Co., Bryn Mawr, Pa.   All Rights Reserved   International Copyright Secured
114-40369   ;Printed in U.S.A.

Unauthorized copying, arranging, adapting or recording is an infringement
of copyright. Infringers are liable under the law.

Used by permission of the publisher.

Chamber Music IV

Ritual series for percussion ensemble (7 players)

Robert Suderburg

I. Waves
II. Symmetries
III. Lyrics

"the distant bells light the air with breathless hope"

Commissioned by The University of Michigan Percussion Ensemble
Charles Owen, Director
Recorded for Columbia Records by The University of Michigan Percussion Ensemble

© 1979 by
Theodore Presser Company

Used By Permission of The Publisher

CHAMBER MUSIC IV

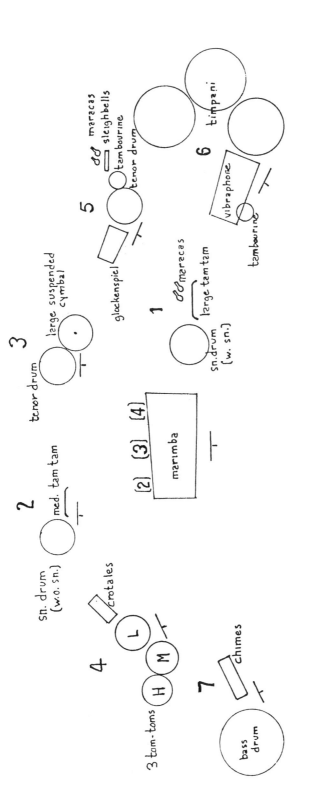

conductor

© 1979 Theodore Presser Company

Used By Permission of The Publisher

Chamber Music IV
Ritual series for percussion ensemble

Score

Duration: ca. 13 minutes

I. WAVES

ROBERT SUDERBURG
(1975)

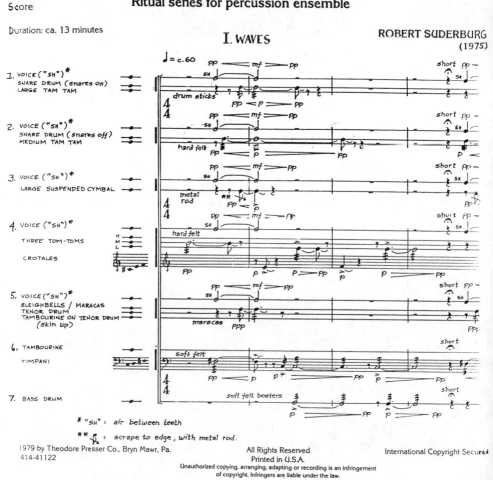

* "SH": air between teeth

** : scrape to edge, with metal rod.

1979 by Theodore Presser Co., Bryn Mawr, Pa.
414-41122

All Rights Reserved
Printed in U.S.A.
Unauthorized copying, arranging, adapting or recording is an infringement
of copyright. Infringers are liable under the law.

International Copyright Secured

Used by permission of the publisher.

PLAYER 1:
Snare Drum, Maracas,
Large Tam-Tam

Chamber Music IV
Ritual series for percussion ensemble

ROBERT SUDERBURG
I. WAVES
(1975)

\# "SH" : air between teeth

© 1979 by Theodore Presser Co., Bryn Mawr, Pa.   All Rights Reserved   International Copyright Secured
414-41122   Printed in U.S.A.
Unauthorized copying, arranging, adapting or recording is an infringement
of copyright. Infringers are liable under the law.

Used by permission of the publisher.

2

PLAYER 2:
Snare Drum,
Medium Tam-Tam,
Marimba

Chamber Music IV
Ritual series for percussion ensemble

ROBERT SUDERBURG
1975

ROBERT SUDERBURG
(1975)

I. WAVES

* "SH" : air between teeth

© 1979 by Theodore Presser Co., Bryn Mawr, Pa.
414-41122

All Rights Reserved
Printed in U.S.A.
Unauthorized copying, arranging, adapting or recording is an infringement
of copyright. Infringers are liable under the law.

International Copyright Secured

Used by permission of the publisher.

PLAYER 3:
Tenor Drum, Marimba,
Large Suspended Cymbal

Chamber Music IV
Ritual series for percussion ensemble
I. WAVES

ROBERT SUDERBURG *
(1975)

\# "SH" : air between teeth

** : scrape to edge, with metal rod

© 1979 by Theodore Presser Co., Bryn Mawr, Pa.   All Rights Reserved   International Copyright Secured
414-41122   Printed in U.S.A.
Unauthorized copying, arranging, adapting or recording is an infringement
of copyright. Infringers are liable under the law.

Used by permission of the publisher.

Chamber Music IV
Ritual series for percussion ensemble
I. WAVES

ROBERT SUDERBURG
(1975)

* "SH" : air between teeth

© 1979 by Theodore Presser Co., Bryn Mawr, Pa.
414-41122

All Rights Reserved
Printed in U.S.A.

International Copyright Secured

Unauthorized copying, arranging, adapting or recording is an infringement
of copyright. Infringers are liable under the law.

Used by permission of the publisher.

PLAYER 5:
Tenor Drum, Glockenspiel,
Tambourine, Sleigh Bells,
Maracas

Chamber Music IV
Ritual series for percussion ensemble

I. WAVES

ROBERT SUDERBURG
(1975)

* "SH" : air between teeth

© 1979 by Theodore Presser Co., Bryn Mawr, Pa.   All Rights Reserved   International Copyright Secured
414-41122   Printed in U.S.A.
Unauthorized copying, arranging, adapting or recording is an infringement
of copyright. Infringers are liable under the law.

Used by permission of the publisher.

© 1979 by Theodore Presser Co., Bryn Mawr, Pa.   All Rights Reserved   International Copyright Secured
414-41122   Printed in U.S.A.
Unauthorized copying, arranging, adapting or recording is an infringement
of copyright. Infringers are liable under the law.

Used by permission of the publisher.

PLAYER 7:
Bass Drum,
Chimes

Chamber Music IV
Ritual series for percussion ensemble

ROBERT SUDERBURG
(1975)

I. WAVES

© 1979 by Theodore Presser Co., Bryn Mawr, Pa.   All Rights Reserved   International Copyright Secured
414-41122   Printed in U.S.A.
Unauthorized copying, arranging, adapting or recording is an infringement
of copyright. Infringers are liable under the law.

Used by permission of the publisher.

4. ALLEN BRINGS

Whether using the traditional system of Western notation as in the accompanying example from my *Quintet* for two violins, viola and two cellos or occasionally adopting more unusual, contemporary systems as in my *Sound Pieces* for voices and noises, I have always tried to present the reader or performer with a vivid image of what I want the music to sound like together with, where feasible, concise directions as to how to make it sound that way. The reader or performer who integrates every note, every dynamic and tempo indication, every articulation mark within his interpretation of the score will have little doubt how I intended each individual tone to sound but even each phrase to flow from one to the other and therefore to relate to one another. I would go so far as to say that an adequate understanding of the overall shape of many of my compositions, not to speak of the way in which successive phrases contribute to that shape, can be obtained merely by plotting the dynamic markings as if on a graph.

Rather than allowing traditional notation to inhibit my musical expression, I have, in fact, accepted some of its constraints in order to help make my compositions more direct, less ambiguous in expression. The only principal disadvantage I have found in it is in conveying just how to allow *tempi* to "bend," a practice difficult enough to convey through imitation but impossible, I suspect, through any system of notation. Although such flexibility of tempo is important in effectively interpreting much of my music, I considered it so crucial in understanding my *Quintet* that I thought it wise to append an explanation to the score, an explanation which I felt would be understood by those who have already attained a better than ordinary understanding of the music of such masters as Beethoven and Chopin.

ALLEN BRINGS
Professor of Music
Queens College, CUNY
New York, NY

To the memory of my parents

Quintet
for
2 Violins, Viola & 2 Violoncelli

Allen Brings

The following scale of dynamic levels should be observed in the
performance of this composition: (ppp), pp, più p, p, poco p,
mp, mf, poco f, f, più f, ff.

© 1980 Allen Brings

MIRA MUSIC ASSOCIATES
199 Mountain Road
Wilton, Connecticut 06897

Used by permission.

Although every effort has been made to indicate clearly pitch, rhythm, dynamics, and articulation in this quintet, it has been possible—because of the limits of our system of notation—to prescribe its tempo requirements only minimally. To determine the appropriate pace of this piece, observing the metronome settings should be regarded only as a first step.

In the slow sections of flexible *tempo rubato* should prevail even where it is not specified in the score. Indeed it is an essential component which contributes to the shape of each phrase and ultimately to the shape of each section.

Each of the fast sections may be understood as comprising the exposition, with its two groups of themes, and development sections of sonata form. Both sections at various times gather a momentum that exceeds the original tempo before retracting. The building of momentum must seem natural and inevitable; it should not be impeded.

©1980 Allen Brings. MIRA MUSIC ASSOCIATES. 199 Mountain Road. Wilton, Connecticut 06897

II. KITCHEN SOUNDS

Text by David S. Walker

Music by Allen Brings

Performance notes for *II. KITCHEN SOUNDS*

To enhance the antiphonal effects in this piece, performers should be arranged in two groups at either end of a long table, as shown in the diagram below.

At each end of the table are the kitchen instruments, and, if possible, a microphone to amplify their sounds. The mixer, if used, should be placed in front of (therefore hidden by) the conductor, so that its sound will come as a surprise.

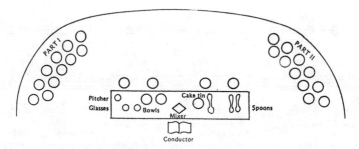

Each member of the speech chorus should hold the required piece of aluminum foil so that it can be seen by the audience – to encourage speculation as to its purpose.

Just before the downbeat, the conductor signals the player of the glasses to tune his instrument

by filling the glasses to the prescribed levels from a pitcher.

Both performers and conductor should use appropriate facial expressions and gestures to help convey the meaning of the music and the text, but not to distract from it.

From *Soundpieces* © Copyright 1974, Shawnee Press, Inc., Delaware Water Gap, PA 18327. International Copyright Secured. All rights reserved. Reprinted with permission.

4

II. KITCHEN SOUNDS

for Keira

(2-part speaking chorus and kitchen utensils)

DAVID S. WALKER

ALLEN BRINGS

I hear
Some kitchen sounds:
Beating, mixing, whirling.
Then later I begin to smell
Cookies!

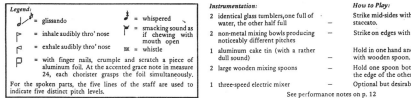

Legend:

♩ = glissando

P = inhale audibly thro' nose

ᑭ = exhale audibly thro' nose

ᑭ = with finger nails, crumple and scratch a piece of aluminum foil. At the accented grace note in measure 24, each chorister grasps the foil simultaneously.

For the spoken parts, the five lines of the staff are used to indicate five distinct pitch levels.

= whispered

= smacking sound as if chewing with mouth open

= whistle

Instrumentation:

2 identical glass tumblers, one full of water, the other half full

2 non-metal mixing bowls producing noticeably different pitches

1 aluminum cake tin (with a rather dull sound)

2 large wooden mixing spoons

1 three-speed electric mixer

How to Play:

Strike mid-sides with teaspoon, gently but staccato.

Strike on edges with wooden spoon.

Hold in one hand and strike center bottom with wooden spoon.

Hold one spoon bottom up; strike it with the edge of the other.

Optional but desirable.

See performance notes on p. 12

(E-154)

From *Soundpieces* © Copyright 1974, Shawnee Press, Inc., Delaware Water Gap, PA 18327. International Copyright Secured. All rights reserved. Reprinted with permission.

II. Kitchen Sounds

Text by David S. Walker   Music by Allen Brings

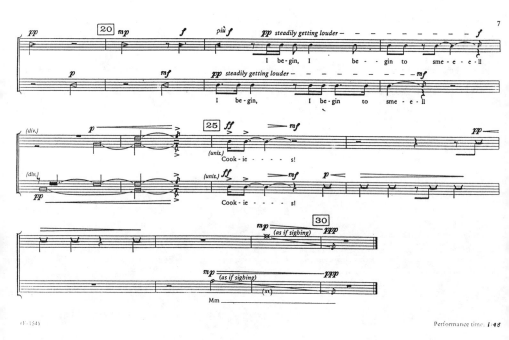

From *Soundpieces* © Copyright 1974, Shawnee Press, Inc., Delaware Water Gap, PA 18327. International Copyright Secured. All rights reserved. Reprinted with permission.

5. JOHN CAGE

ATLAS ECLIPTICALIS

General Directions

Each part has 4 pages. Each page has 5 systems. Space horizontally equals time as indicated by a conductor who performs a circle like that of a watch-hand. The four arrows of each system correspond to the 0″, 15″, 30″, and 45″ indications of the conductor. The fifth at 60″ completes the system. The conductor's time will be at least twice as slow as clock time.

Space vertically equals frequency. Equal space is given each chromatic tone. Conventional points are marked ♯, ♭ or ♮. The absence of such signs means that the tones are not at conventional points; the player is to use his eye with respect to the space to determine his action.

Events are single tones or aggregates-in-time (constellations). Two numbers above an event (or near it) tell: the first, how many notes are as short as possible; the second, how many have appreciable duration. The absence of numbers means all tones are as short as possible. A ⌢ means all have some duration. This may not exceed that of a breath or of a bow.

Within an aggregate, space need not refer to time. Individual tones of an aggregate may appear in any succession. In parts permitting the playing of two or more at once (string and percussion parts) the player is free to make such combinations. He may also make interpenetrations of tones (e.g. producing a pizz. during the bowing of a tone, hitting an instrument during the resonance of another, etc.).

A silence takes place between tones, even two of the same aggregate, unless they are superimposed or interpenetrate. Melodic lines are not produced by the players individually. The player is under no obligation to play tones in rapid succession.

The loudness of tones is relative to their size. Thus, most tones are played softly. No tones are to be played intermittently, nor is tone production extraordinary. Repetitions of tones within an aggregate may be made if the stem connecting the tones crosses through a note. In such a case, the repetition (if made) should follow intervening tones, and be short (if previously long) or long (if previously short).

Where changes are made from one instrument to another (e.g. from oboe to

Copyright ©1961 by Henmar Press Inc., 373 Park Avenue South, New York, N.Y. 10016. Reprinted by permission.

171

English horn, or from trumpet in B^b to one in D), make the change following the completion of an aggregate.

A performance may be at any point between minimum activity (silence) and maximum activity.

Directions for Percussion

Each part has four pages. Each page has five systems. Space horizontally equals time as indicated by a conductor who performs a circle like that of a watch-hand. The arrows of each system correspond to the 0″, 15″, 30″, 45″ and 60″ indications of the conductor. The conductor's time will be at least twice as slow as clocktime.

The percussion parts graph the physical location of available instruments. These are placed in a semi-circle around the performer, are various, as numerous as possible, and not arranged according to relative pitch or timbre. The single line of the staff corresponds to straight—forward, below—to the left, above—to the right.

Events are single sounds or aggregates-in-time (constellations). Two numbers associated with an event tell: the first, how many notes are as short as possible; the second, how many have appreciable duration. The absence of numbers means all tones are as short as possible. A ⌒ means all have some duration. Sounds having length are rolls, fricative sounds, l.v., etc.

Within an aggregate, space need not refer to time. Sounds of an aggregate may appear in any succession. Two or more may sound at once—be superimposed—or they may interpenetrate—one occurring during the resonance of another.

A silence takes place between sounds, even of the same aggregate, unless they are superimposed or interpenetrate. The player is under no obligation to play sounds in rapid succession.

The loudness of sounds is relative to their size. Most sounds are played softly.

Avoid noise-makers suggestive of specific things, beings or events. A tape machine (if tapes provided by the composer are available) or electronic instrument may be used.

Cartridges may be used. When the object inserted in the cartridge is changed, make such change following the completion of an aggregate (gain on the associated amplifier reduced to zero).

Repetitions of sounds within an aggregate may be made if the stem connecting the notes crosses through one of them. Such repetition (if made) should follow intervening sounds, and be short (if previously long) or long (if previously short).

A performance may be at any point between minimum activity (silence) and maximum activity (what's written).

Directions for Conductor and Assistant

The conductor determines the length of a performance, and how much and which part of the composition—the same for all players—is to be performed. A system equals at least 2 minutes—preferably more. (Extend the time to the point where the presence of silence is felt.) The conductor, however, performs a single clock-cycle for each system. At 0″, 30″, and 60″ he makes changes of arm, at 15″ and 45″ changes of palm. From the last 30″ to the end at 60″, he uses both arms, fingers touching at the conclusion.

As many instruments as possible are to be equipped with contact microphones. These are connected to individual amplification systems and thence to individual loudspeakers. An assistant to the conductor prepares his own part from "Cartridge Music" for the operation of the dials (gain and tone control). Where the amplifiers exceed 20, he makes a drawing of the same size as those of "Cartridge Music" but having that number of shapes that there are amplifiers. Notes within shapes are gain, outside, tone control.

The composing means involved I-Ching operations together with the placing of transparent templates on the pages of an astronomical atlas and inscribing the positions of stars. I am grateful to Richard K. Winslow and to Toshi Ichiyanagi for assistance in the preparation of the parts.

J.C.   New London, Connecticut   7/21/61

ATLAS ECLIPTICALIS

CELLO 7

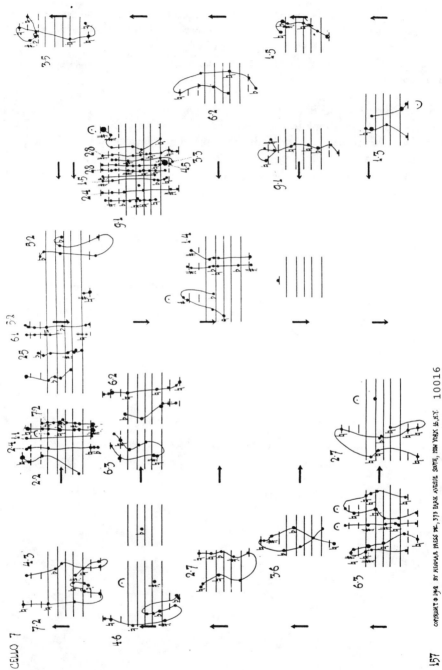

Used by Permission.

COPYRIGHT © 1962 BY HENMAR PRESS INC., 373 PARK AVENUE SOUTH, NEW YORK 16, N.Y. 10016

6. JOHN HOWARD

NOTATION

If I could briefly describe my position with regard to the notation of my compositions, I would do so under the following three headings:

1. Control
2. Freedom
3. Invention

I am prepared to use pre-existent ("traditional") forms of notation in my music, & tend to do so where a certain kind of metrical control is implied. You might say that my "traditional" notation conforms to the extended version now generally accepted in new music: for instance, scores are usually notated at pitch, accelerando figures are written out in the following way:

and the music often contains decorating figures which are notated outside, as it were, the metrical framework.

By freedom, I mean that my music is often non-metrical, and as a result I tend to use the accepted forms of proportional or "space-time" notation. It is quite possible in my music for textures to contain both metred and proportional notation at once. (The accompanying example, the opening of my Symphony for Chamber Orchestra, illustrates this sort of combined approach.)

Finally, I regard it as important for me to be inventive in my choices of notation, both because, at times, notation can be a stimulus to the performer, and because the forging of new kinds of musical language must go hand-in-hand with the invention of new ways of expressing them in visual symbols.

JOHN HOWARD
Principal lecturer in Music
Kingston Polytechnic
Kingston, Surrey, England

Symphony for Chamber Orchestra

7. ROGER SESSIONS

NOTES ON PERFORMANCE

Divertimento

Metronomic indications are to be considered as approximative and are to be inter-preted flexibly within fairly narrow limits. When a change of tempo is indicated in exact terms, i.e. for example ♩ = ♩ or ⌐³¬ ♪ = ♩ it is to be scrupulously observed. The values thus indicated always straddle the bar line and each of the values indicated applies to the measure directly under which it occurs.

The division into measures and beats is structural, but not accentual, in intent; neither the first beat, or any beat of the measure is to be accented unless such accentuation is expressly indicated.

Dynamic gradations are to be considered within the context of the general categories of *piano* and *forte*; in the following order, from soft to loud:

ppp, pp, p molto, p, mp;

mf, poco f, f, f molto, ff, fff

They indicate values not absolute, but relative to the context in which they occur. The indications *mp* and *mf* may be in this sense roughly equivalent; but if they occur in sequence or in close succession, *mf* is to be considered slightly stronger than *mp*.

Such terms as *tranquillo, agitato*, and *animato*, which do not in themselves carry any widely recognized specific implication of tempo are to be taken as referring rather to the *manner*, than the *tempo* of *performance*, unless specific indications of tempo accom-pany them.

The term *animando*, however, generally implies an increase in tempo, in support of the desired increase in animation. Distinction should likewise be made between the term *ritenuto*—holding back—on the one hand, and *ritardando* and *rallentando* on the other; the latter terms are used to imply a more gradual slackening of speed.

Such terms as *allegro, vivace, andante*, and *adagio*, etc., have acquired precise conventional meanings and are to be taken in their usual sense.

Here as elsewhere in the composer's work, the following marks of articulation are used:

©1977 Merion Music, Inc. Used by permission of the publisher.

· (staccato sign)—short, light staccato
▾ (stroke)—very short, sharp staccato
͞· staccato, but held long enough for developed tone
— (tenuto)—tone held to its full value, without "decay" unless specifically
indicated, but not *legato*

A slur added to any of these signs indicates smoothness of execution and phrasing.
A slur binding a note to a rest indicates that the note is to be held to its full length,
with unchanged dynamic intensity unless otherwise indicated.
Marks of accentuation:

> indicates a sharp attack, with only such stress as results therefrom
ʌ indicates perceptible and strong stress, always in terms of the mode of
articulation (legato, staccato, tenuto) otherwise indicated
< > indicates perceptible stress achieved by a soft attack followed by "bearing
down" on the note instead of attacking it sharply
sf indicates strong stress within the dynamic content in which it occurs
sff indicates the strongest possible stress, regardless of context

DIVERTIMENTO
for orchestra
I. Prelude

to Carl Haverlin

Full Score

ROGER SESSIONS
(1960)

Allegro, un poco maestoso (♩ = 100)

Piccolo
Flutes 1 2
Oboe
English Horn
Clarinet (B♭)
Bass Clarinet (B♭)
Bassoons 1 2
Horns (F) 1 2
Trumpets (B♭) 1 2
Trombones 1 2
Tuba
Timpani
Percussion
Vibraphone Xylophone
Piano

Allegro, un poco maestoso (♩ = 100)

Violins I II
Violas
Violoncelli
Contrabasses

© 1977 by Merion Music, Inc., Bryn Mawr, Pa.
Theodore Presser Co., Sole Representative
446-41037

All Rights Reserved
Printed in U. S. A.

Unauthorized copying, arranging, adapting or recording is an infringement of copyright. Infringers are liable under the law.

International Copyright Secured
This edition published 1982

Used by permission of the publisher.

8. HUBERT BIRD

REGARDING MY NOTATIONAL PROCEDURE

In the preparation of all music manuscript I am most concerned that everything about it be as clear and "camera-ready" as possible. There are several reasons for this. For one, I believe one's own professional status is reflected in the kind of care given to one's manuscript. For another, clarity cuts down on possible wasted rehearsal time—which, in turn, translates to wasted dollars—truly a "professional" consideration! For yet another, when submitting manuscripts to conductors for consideration for programming, when submitting works to be judged in competitions and also when submitting them to publishers for publication-consideration, I cannot help but think that good, clear manuscript has to have a positive influence on those who review it for whatever purposes. (One expects the musical content to be substantive!)

Though in the past I have used the time-honored Ozalid ("onion-skin") process for copying scores and parts, in recent years I have found duplex xerography (Xerox copying on both sides of a single sheet) to be much easier and faster. Today, therefore, my procedure for copying includes the making of my own manuscript paper to order for whatever copying job is being undertaken at the moment, combined with the use of very simple (and quite readily available) pens—usually of the "felt-tip" variety—along with a bottle of "liquid paper" (or "white out"). For lettering of titles, etc., I have recently adopted the rub-on, transfer letters available from most print shops. Once master copies of scores and parts are completed, reproduction by xerography along with the common "plastic comb" binding with "leatherette" covers provides a finished product that is very professional-looking and represents the composer in the best possible manner.

As far as the actual musical notation itself is concerned, though I have experimented fairly extensively in the past with a number of notational techniques including graphic notation, "cut-away" scores, etc., I have determined that, for myself, the standard notational procedures of the past are adequate for my needs. I have adopted, however, the relatively recent procedure of notating time-signatures with a note shown on the bottom, rather than a number. It seems to me this communicates more accurately and quickly than the time-honored number representing a notational value.

HUBERT BIRD
Professor of Music
Keene State College
Keene, NH

THREE BIBLICAL SONGS

to Drs. Paul and Jean Blacketon
and
Mrs. Earlene Fitch

I. O LORD, THOU HAST SEARCHED
ME AND KNOWN ME

© Copyright 1987 by Hubert C. Bird
International Copyright Secured
ALL RIGHTS RESERVED

Used by permission.

2.

QUINTET FOR BRASS
IN FIVE MOVEMENTS
I. ALLEGRO MODERATO

HUBERT BIRD

© Copyright 1987 by Hubert C. Bird. Used by permission.

9. LOU HARRISON

SUITE FOR SYMPHONIC STRINGS

Introductory Notes

The parts for each section of players had ought to divide by the half-chair, that is, the outer player should play part 1, & the inner, part 2. In this score I have used as the extremes, in the notation of dynamics, only the *pp*, & the *ff*; but these should be taken to mean "barely audible" and "the loudest possible" (that is compatible with good playing). As a result, I've resorted to such notations as *p.*, or *f.*, *molto—piu p.*, or *f* etc. which should be clear enough in their contexts. The special dynamic & rhythmic decline at the end of the Lament (#5) will take planning & practice. At the place marked, a "tempo-of-Ritard" plus a "degreeing-of-Dimin." had ought to begin, which, by steady progress, arrives inexorably at the final silence. Both must begin right, in order that the end be inevitable. The violinists Stefan Krayle & Richard Dee have given me kind help in the matter of bowings concerned with grace notes, which, I understand, bow best with the note to which they lead. All other bowings are my own, and if they are not good, then change them. As always, I put my trust in the excellence of my fellow musicians, for many of my pieces have much profited from their help.

My diacritical marks should be construed so: the usual accent mark (>) is meant to indicate a sharp attack, & often louder than the surrounding notes. It is *not* detached, though, unless combined with the mark of staccato. The "Louré" mark (–) I use to mean "pushed a little" & does not refer to bowing, nor, again, detachment, unless it is also so marked. In melodies the accent marks are rhythmic subdivisions & not dramatically used. In order to give this idea greater clarity I present here the notation of a passage from Variation III in the Canonic Variations (the "response"-phrase) as it appears in my original notation of the movement:

©1961 by C.F. Peters Corporation, 373 Park Avenue South, New York, NY 10016. Used by permission.

As you can see, it looks (compositionally) much clearer this way. Still it had to be put in order for musicians to play. Well, then, the accents which appear in the full score are meant to show where the little "melodicles" are, in the resilience of the full melodies.

You will notice, too, that I've "written-out" every last grace note, in the full score. (I see that I've done this in the Ductia #4 too, so that these remarks apply to it as well.) Hence, in this movement, every thirty-second note is part of a grace. I did this to make clear that I want all the grace notes to be rhythmic, and not at all that minute trill (which has been given me when I haven't written them out, or have forgotten to make a note about the matter, or haven't been at rehearsals to explain. In any event, it was stimulating to me to write them all out for once, & I hope that it won't make playing the movement very much harder. Other graces in this Suite are to be played rhythmically too, & *before* the beat, as here. So much for the mysterious appearance of what are very simple passages.

At the 1960 Institute of Orchestral Studies of the American Symphony Orchestra League, under the aegis of the Rockefeller Foundation, & held during that summer at Asilomar in California, I had the fortune to make a study directly with the orchestra; and I found out, through the goodwill of the splendid musicians there present, exactly what the sounds for which I've scored in the lower strings do sound like. These new methods, then, are well, and generously prepared. We found that with 2 or 3 fingers beaten here the Contra-Bassi emit a sonorous "drumming."

*The cello section of The Louisville Orchestra used Guitar picks instead of fingernails & I much liked the sound. I think that Grace Whitney invented this good device.

Copyright © 1961 by
C. F. Peters Corporation
New York 16, N. Y.
International Copyright Secured.
All Rights Reserved.

10. GUNTHER SCHULLER

SYMPHONY
For Brass and Percussion

I

Gunther Schuller
(Op. 16)

Andante(♩=66 - 69)

espr.

© Copyright MCMLIX, Malcolm Music, Ltd. International Copyright Secured. All Rights Reserved. Sole Selling Agent: Shawnee Press Inc., Delaware Water Gap, PA 18327. U.S. copyright renewed. Reprinted with permission.

BIBLIOGRAPHY

Ammer, Christine. *Musician's Handbook of Foreign Terms*. New York; London: G. Schirmer, Inc., 1971.
A small but very helpful book containing about 2,700 foreign expression marks and directions as well as instructions for pronunciation.

Apel, Willi. *Harvard Dictionary of Music*. Cambridge, Mass.: The Belknap Press of Harvard University Press, 1972.
A large, authoritative and well-respected dictionary of music.

Cope, David. *New Music Composition*. New York: Schirmer Books; London: Collier-Macmillan, 1977.
Information is comprehensive yet clear and direct. Each chapter deals with different aspects of techniques, ideas and instrumentation. Included are fine examples to illustrate a point in new music. In addition, there are assignments for classroom use. It is suggested that two semesters could be the time span to cover the twenty-seven chapters. There is a list of works for further study.

Cope, David. *New Music Notation*. Dubuque, Iowa: Kendall/Hunt Publishing Company, 1976.
An excellent book on the subject of practical new notations. Part one discusses developments in new music notation. Part two deals with suggested symbols. The author suggests the practice of adding to traditional notation rather than creating completely new systems; e.g., using old symbols, new standardized symbols and verbal directions. Included are useful charts for the choice of symbols.

Cundick, Robert, and Dayley, Newell. *Music Manuscript*. Orem, Utah: Sonos Music Resources, Inc., 1971, 1974.
A simple, very short but practical guide for traditional nota-

tion. It gives explicit directions of the actual drawing of fundamental symbols, such as clefs, notes, flags, etc., as well as instructions on how to use pens and other drawing aids. It deals briefly with layouts and reproduction of manuscripts.

Dallin, Leon. *Techniques of Twentieth Century Composition.* Dubuque, Iowa: William C. Brown Company, 1957, 1964.
Important styles, procedures, materials and techniques are discussed. Examples of music of well-known composers are made more readable by using only the treble and bass clefs. Orchestral scores are reduced and transposed. Assignments are suggested for the student at the end of each chapter. Traditional terminology is used as much as possible.

Donato, Anthony. *Preparing Music Manuscript.* Englewood Cliffs, N.J.: Prentice-Hall, 1970, 1952.
This guide deals mainly with traditional notation and layout procedures. Examples and illustrations are very clear. In addition, there is information on reproduction, binding, proofreading and copyrights. There is an appendix with degrees of the scale, names of instruments and voices, ranges of instruments and voices, some directions for instruments and foreign musical terms.

Johnson, Harold M., *How to Write Music Manuscript.* New York: Carl Fischer, Inc., 1946.
An exercise-method handbook for the music student, copyist, arranger, composer, teacher.

Karkoschka, Erhard. *Notation in New Music: (A Critical Guide to Interpretation and Realization).* New York; Washington: Praeger, 1972. Translated from the German edition by Ruth Koenig (*Das Schriftbild der neuen Musik*), 1966 by Moeck Verlag, Celle/FRG. This translation was published with the cooperation of Universal Edition, Vienna and London.
This is a survey of new music notation and its problems. The development of new notation is encouraged. The book is divided into three parts:
1) discussion of the situation at the time that the book was written;
2) presentation of new symbols;

3) presentation of notational examples of new notational systems from known composers with accompanying explanation.

Kennan, Kent Wheeler. *The Technique of Orchestration.* Englewood Cliffs, N.J.: Prentice-Hall, 1970, 1952.

Extremely useful guide, particularly to professionals and students in the areas of composing, arranging and conducting. it deals with each kind of instrument, special devices, orchestral practice and scoring. Suggestions for assignments and listening are helpful. Included are excellent examples. There are lists of foreign names for instruments and orchestral terms, and a chart for ranges of instruments.

The New Grove Dictionary of Music and Musicians. Ed. by Stanley Sadie. London: Macmillan, 1980.

The distinguished and definitive encyclopedia consisting of twenty volumes.

Rachlin, Harvey. *The Songwriter's Handbook.* New York: Funk and Wagnalls, 1977.

This is a valuable guide and reference book for songwriters, covering areas such as the creation and selling of a song, auditions, arrangers, business information, reproduction, performing rights organizations, markets (film, night club, recordings, etc.), music publishers.

Read, Gardner. *Music Notation.* New York: Taplinger, 1968, 1979.

A very comprehensive, authoritative and well-illustrated book with excellent material. Each chapter ends with sections headed "Modern Innovations" and "Notation Exercises" which are very helpful. In addition, there are many fine charts. This is a book to keep in one's library.

Risatti, Howard. *New Music Vocabulary.* Urbana; Chicago; London: University of Illinois Press, 1975.

A valuable reference book because of the number of symbols included. It does not attempt to guide the reader in selecting the symbol.

Roemer, Clinton. *The Art of Music Copying.* Sherman Oaks, Cal.: Roerick Music Company, 1973.
This practical manual is particularly useful to a copyist who prepares music manuscripts for films, television, recordings and night club acts. It is helpful, as well, in preparing all other kinds of music manuscripts.

Warfield, Gerald. *Index of New Musical Notation (Writings on Contemporary Music Notation: An Annotated Bibliography)*, MLA Index and Bibliography Series, Number 16. Ann Arbor, MI: Music Library Association, 1976.
An important book of listings of writings on new notations. The annotations are of help.

INDEX